MEMORY
in
MIND and BRAIN

═══════

What
Dream Imagery
Reveals

═══════

MORTON F. REISER

BasicBooks
A Division of HarperCollins*Publishers*

Library of Congress Cataloging-in-Publication Data
Reiser, Morton F., 1919–
    Memory in mind and brain : what dream imagery
reveals / Morton Reiser.
        p.   cm.
    Includes bibliographical references and index.
    ISBN 0-465-04605-3
    1. Memory.   2. Dreams.   3. Imagery (Psychology)
        4. Mind and body.   5. Psychoanalysis.
            6. Neurobiology.   I. Title.
BF371.R375   1990   90-55662
153.1'2–dc20   CIP

For information about our audio products, write us at:
Newbridge Book Clubs, 3000 Cindel Drive, Delran, NJ   08370

For Lynn again

companion,
tracking on her own
close by and ready
to stop and listen
  teach and learn
  advise
  edit

and share the game

Contents

CONTENTS

List of Illustrations

Acknowledgments

I am indebted to many individuals and institutions for assistance and support. Special thanks are due to investigators to whom I turned for advice and consultation: Floyd Bloom, William Bunney, Monte Buchsbaum, Mardi Horowitz, Eric Kandel, Michael Gazzaniga, Bruce McEwen, Stuart Zola Morgan, and Larry Squire. All of them gave freely of their time in discussion, and provided opportunities to visit and observe in their laboratories. A three-month fellowship at The Neurosciences Institute at Rockefeller University provided time for intensive study and for highly valuable discussions with its director, Gerald Edelman, that broadened and deepened my appreciation of the opportunities informed science can offer for understanding the complexities of mind/brain. I also was privileged to spend long hours of study, observation, and discussion in the laboratory of Jonathan Winson. His influence in shaping some of the ideas recounted in this book will be obvious. As part of the fellowship I had the opportunity, with the help of W. Einar Gall, research director of the Institute, to organize and conduct a productive and stimulating two-day conference on Memory and Dreams. I am indebted to all of the participants for contributions to the conference, ideas that helped to shape the subsequent development of my thinking about memory and dreams: Rosalind Cartwright, Eric Kandel, Mortimer Mishkin, Patricia Goldman-Rakic, Howard Roffwarg, Daniel Schacter, Howard Shevrin, and Jonathan Winson. I want especially also to thank Mortimer Mishkin and Howard Roffwarg for reading the manuscript of this book and offering critical advice and suggestions as well as encouragement.

I thank the Rockefeller Foundation for a two-month Resident Fellowship at their Conference and Study Center at Bellagio, Italy, which provided ideal conditions and environment for drafting the initial stages of the manuscript.

Discussions with fellow members of Group 4 of the Center for Advanced Psychoanalytic Studies at Princeton were helpful in refining some of the psychoanalytic ideas as they developed in the course of writing the book.

Very special appreciation is due to Marshall Edelson and to Lynn Whisnant Reiser, both of whom, as before, served as indefatigable consultants throughout many versions. In their own special ways each of them provided steady encouragement as well as intellectual enrichment of ideas and text.

My thanks too to Phyllis Gibson, my secretary, for her patience, understanding, and persistence throughout, and for cogent references to literary sources, particularly from the theater. Jo Ann Miller, Director of Professional Books and Senior Editor at Basic Books, provided helpful counsel, and I am grateful to her. Finally, I wish to acknowledge my appreciation to Harriet Phillips and Ann E. Armas for taking time out from their regular duties to help in the final stages of manuscript preparation; and to Virginia Simon for her skill and understanding in preparing the drawings and diagrams.

Permission to reproduce previously published illustrations has been granted by the following publishers and authors: Tim Appenzeller, Peter J. Hauri, Ph.D., Hoyle Leigh, M.D., Mortimer Mishkin, Ph.D., Cambridge University Press, Plenum Publishing Corporation, the Royal Society of London, *Scientific American,* and the Upjohn Company.

We can never know
what is out there:
the real stuff of the universe
what it is doing, and why

We can never know
what is in there:
the real stuff of our beings
what it is doing, and why

But
these are what we want most
  to know

Sensing
from without
and within
impressions filtered through
  senses, sensibilities,
    brains,
  feelings, memories, and dreams,
  language, and metaphor
we think
  we know

General Introduction

Nature keeps the secret of dreams filed in a safe deposit box. As with all such boxes, two keys are required to open it, but these are special keys in that they also provide access to two file cabinets. One of the keys unlocks a file containing neurobiologic and cognitive neuroscientific information about memory. The other unlocks a different file, this one containing clinical psychoanalytic information, also about memory. Any one of us is allowed to use either key whenever and for as long as we want, but only one at a time. Yet the secret in the safe deposit box, which I will refer to as *mind/brain*, encompasses both sets of information in a unitary form that we can only imagine. Never having both keys at the same time, we can never unlock it, never really know what it is. What follows in this book is an account of things I have learned in the course of my attempts to figure out what may be in the safe deposit box and what that unitary form could possibly be.

This volume will present the results of a study that developed quite naturally from prior explorations into more general clinical and empirical issues displayed in mind/brain-body functions. It

1

represents a phase of my broader ongoing inquiry into the question of how the mind works—and how the brain enables it to do what it does. In fact, this book is a sequel to an earlier volume (Reiser 1984). In focusing on dreams and memory as illustrative phenomena, it demonstrates the use of a particular approach (the dual-track approach discussed in chapter 1) to the study of phenomena that are simultaneously manifest in the separate domains of mind and body. This study is a more penetrating and focused inquiry than I had undertaken before, looking now specifically into psychoanalytic and neurobiologic aspects of memory, particularly as manifest in the dream. The dream process offers a particularly promising area for inquiry, because it reflects both mind and brain-body mechanisms and is accessible to parallel study by research methods appropriate to each—sometimes separately, sometimes together. Even so, formidable conceptual obstacles stand in the way of achieving a truly integrated understanding through the study of data that illuminate dual aspects of unitary phenomena. These conceptual problems and suggested ways of dealing with them have been discussed at length in previous publications (Edelson 1984, 1988; Reiser 1984). I will discuss these problems again in connection with specific issues as the text unfolds (particularly in chapters 2, 4, and 10).

There is another problem. An increasingly large number of disciplines are now involved in studying the nervous system and behavior. As technology advances, scientists in each discipline tend more and more to look at particular (often highly specialized) aspects of mind and/or brain function. As a result, terminologies, conceptual models, and theories are becoming increasingly diverse as they adapt to and reflect specialized research interests. Even though most investigators working in the general area share a broad common interest in the mind, effective collaboration and even communication become difficult. Given the advanced degree of subspecialization and the realities of academic and professional life, this difficulty is unavoidable—particularly when one considers that the range of disciplines extends from cell and molecular neurobiology, along with artificial intelligence, at one end to psychoanalysis, along with the social sciences and humanities, at the other. This broad range, which both reflects and enhances progress, surely is not to be decried or interfered with, yet it does come at some cost.

One result can be that investigators tend to look in one file cabinet *or* the other, and after a while they lose interest in the contents of the other. This need not constitute a problem for the individual researcher, but it can be serious for the field as a whole. When different studies address the same phenomena without realizing it, complementary data may go to waste. Nowhere is this more likely to be true than when the studies from two opposite ends of the broad span of disciplines address phenomena that require information from both domains for full understanding. In such instances, recognizing the existence of reciprocally relevant data could contribute to the development of clinical insights and potential research leads.

The work reported here began with the conviction that it would be important first to search out such complementary information as may exist and second to think through the possible implications for an understanding of how the mind—enabled by the brain—may work. I have drawn primarily on empirical data: on the psychoanalytic side, largely from Freud's seminal discoveries and from my own clinical work; on the neurobiologic side, from the work of key investigators, making use of both the published literature and on-site consultation and conferences. Throughout the book quotations from published works of key investigators will be included in order to share with the reader direct exposure to some of the ideas and opinions held by these eyewitness authorities. Fortunately, recent years have been witness to a dazzlingly rapid burgeoning of research that combines cognitive psychological with neurobiological techniques and approaches in the new field of cognitive neuroscience. It will become clear as the story develops that this discipline serves as an appropriate interface between psychoanalysis and neuroscience. The empirical distance from psychoanalysis to cognitive psychology is not really all that great, nor is the empirical distance from cognitive psychology to neurobiology. Both gaps are more readily negotiable than the jump from psychoanalysis to neuroscience, where the asymmetry in the nature of the data on the two sides seems more extreme and therefore more forbidding.

The plan of the book is straightforward. It follows my mental processes on a journey of discovery: from psychoanalytic data and hypotheses about mind to cognitive neuroscience data and inferences about brain, and finally to conclusions and speculations about the interrelationship between mind and brain. Critical points of logic underlying the development of conclusions and speculations will be reviewed in chapter 10, just before the conclusions are presented in chapter 11.

Part I spells out challenging background questions about memory and dreams. Chapters 1 and 2 acquaint the reader with contemporary questions about putative memory and meaning functions of dreaming. As pointed out by Harold Kudler (1989), they are modern restatements of old challenges that Freud addressed in the opening chapter of *The Interpretation of Dreams* (1900). These introductory chapters are designed to stimulate interest in dream phenomena, in Freud's original formulations, and in the challenges and questions offered by some sectors of contemporary cognitive neuroscience and psychophysiology. For example: Can the mind operate in accordance with mutually contradictory principles—is dreaming both for remembering and for forgetting? Do dreams have a memory-processing role in adaptation/survival? Do dreams convey meanings? If so, how? Are the meanings obvious or hidden? What revisions are necessary to bring Freud's theory into line with modern neuroscientific knowledge? Goals and strategies for addressing these challenges are introduced and discussed.

In Part II, clinical psychoanalytic observations are offered to consolidate and extend a functional mental memory principle developed in earlier work (Reiser 1984). That principle states that perceptual residues in the mind are arranged in enduring "nodal memory networks," in which associative links between "images" are based on their potential for evoking the same or highly similar emotions. This principle is then applied in two ways. First, I show retrospectively that it was operant (but not fully explicated) in Freud's classic dream of the botanical monograph. Then I use it to add an additional perspective on a previously observable but not fully appreciated aspect of psychoanalytic process: that a version of the analysand's nodal memory network is encoded into the analyst's memory system and that interactions between cogent sections of the analyst's and the analysand's stores of memories may play an important role in empathy, thereby influencing the course of the analytic process. The second application carries not only clinical importance but methodologic implications for research, both on the psychoanalytic process itself and on the use of psychoanalysis in research on memory.

Part III, the section dealing with brain science, considers the large quantity of empirical data indicating that many functional *brain memory* principles are isomorphic with functional *mind memory* principles such as that concerning nodal memory networks, described above. It is particularly noteworthy that most of the experiments on the brain side were done to investigate other issues; they were not concerned with the contents of the depth psychology drawer of the mind cabinet. The fact that the mental and physiologic data reviewed show correspondence, even though they were generated independently, lends credence to the idea that they can be regarded as complementary.

Finally, in part IV, having reviewed the psychophysiology of REM sleep, an effort is directed toward formulating a balanced contemporary psychobiological model of the dream process. Building on aspects of Freud's model, a theory is presented which, deriving principles from both domains of knowledge, proposes an integrated model of how dream images are formed. The result is promising. It has implications for clinical work with dreams in the psychoanalytic situation and for continuing psychobiological research on this important but still incompletely understood life function.

BACKGROUND CONTEXT: THE PSYCHOLOGICAL FIELD OF INQUIRY

The questions and issues which gave impetus to this work arose from a much broader context than the book itself can encompass: problems such as the question of free will and the difficulty of understanding the nature of consciousness and its interrelationships with perception, memory, and emotion. Here I briefly will share some of the reflections that arose in my mind as these issues were encountered in the course of the work. Since they must have influenced my work, I include these thoughts as a contextual frame and to assist readers in tuning in to a corresponding wavelength.

Anyone sitting down to think through a problem or commit ideas to paper may assume that the process will be fully deliberate, intentional and controlled. Not so! Many novelists report that once they have created characters, the characters take on a life of their own; the author cannot always be certain from day to day how the fictional people will act, or even exactly how the plot may finally develop. To find out, the writer as well as the reader has to wait until the book has been written. There is a passive aspect to the writing experience, almost as if writing, at least in part, is akin to reading—not from the written page for the author, but from within one's own mind. The content becomes fully explicit only when it appears on the printed page.

The same is true of writing nonfiction and scientific reports. In this case, the data to be reported are fixed, but the organization and conceptualization have to evolve before the message fully emerges in final form. Only then is it available for deliberate conscious consideration and critical appraisal. First drafts don't come out exactly the way the writer "intends," and frequently many revisions are necessary before the author is satisfied with the text. The author who creates the work does not, in fact, control the process as fully as the words "think," "create," and "write" usually connote.

The implications of this are profound. Taken together with experimental data on intentionality (Libet 1985) and consciousness in man (Gazzaniga 1989; Edelman 1989), they constitute a major challenge to the idea of, and the cherished belief in, free will.

Freud (1900, chapter 7) conceived of consciousness as a "first system" of the mind (perception-consciousness, pcpt-cs) that functions as a passive perceptual screen registering stimuli impinging upon it, and he postulated that sensitivity of (or access to) the screen was regulated by attention. He postulated further that behind the perception-consciousness system "lies a second system which transforms the momentary excitations of the first system into permanent traces" (1900, p. 538). He realized that the same tissue components of the neural apparatus cannot both register *and* remember stimuli.

> A trace is left in our psychical apparatus of the perceptions which impinge upon it. This we may describe as a "memory trace". . . . But . . . there are obvious difficulties involved in supposing that one and the same system can accurately retain modifications of its elements and yet remain perpetually open to the reception of fresh occasions for modification. (Freud 1900, p. 538)

Larry Squire, a leading contemporary neuropsychologist, comments similarly on the same issue:

> If significant aspects of memory are localized in the processing structures of neocortex, how can cortical processing systems change without altering the nature of perception itself? That is, how can extensive synaptic change occur in cortex, as is required for memory storage, while the cortex has an opposite need to preserve its information-processing functions? (Squire 1987, p. 125)

7

The idea of consciousness as a passive screen combined with the concept of the dynamic unconscious as playing a powerful role in behavior (psychic determinism) certainly shakes to its roots the subjective certainty about conscious control of behavior that we all enjoy.

For the moment let us temporarily accept the idea of psychic determinism, which holds that mental contents and processes that are inaccessible to consciousness may nonetheless remain active in mind/brain and participate in initiating, guiding, and otherwise influencing behavior. For some readers, this may entail suspension of disbelief, but having put it aside for the moment, the issue may not seem so fully polarized as before—perhaps each view can then be seen as partly right and partly wrong. Quite possibly our mind/brains, as complex as they are, can at one and the same time operate in accordance with mutually contradictory principles (Freud 1900, p. 599).

If so, it would be a relief! As I write these lines, I *know* that I'm doing active and deliberate things: thinking thoughts, making decisions, etc. Some days the overflowing wastebasket reveals evidence of repeated decisions to reject what comes out, but eventually I must settle for the closest I can come to clear exposition of ideas that are mine—ideas that have been many years in gestation, and are in my mind, but can, and often do, elude precise verbal expression.

If one remembers that in Freud's scheme it is attention that regulates the sensitivity of the perceptual consciousness screen (pcpt-cs), *it becomes possible to assign an important role to intention without abandoning the idea of the passive perceptual screen.* Picture "pcpt-cs" as a movie screen that registers successive (separate) images replacing each other rapidly enough to be seen as continuous. In a similar way, the subjective experience of a train of thought could in fact be the way we experience a succession of separate ideational representations spaced closely enough to be experienced as continuous. Viewed in this way, intentional control would be exerted indirectly, that is, through regulation of attention, and the scheme would be compatible both with data that tell us consciousness is a passive screen and with commonsense psychology, which insists justifiably that it is much more than that.

If things did work this way, a person deep in thought could be compared to the rider of a spirited, basically wild horse, and thinking would encompass both an active and a passive component. In fact, this is not such a bad metaphor*: one could learn to think and even gain advanced, albeit not complete, mastery of the skill of controlling the process. Perhaps the ability to deploy attention so as to experience a guided "reading" of a sequence of thought images for screening in consciousness is a capacity that developed in the course of evolution. Animals learn and remember—do they experience consciousness? If so, is it the same as in the human? Perhaps the above-postulated ability to guide the content of consciousness (that is, to think in the way we do) is one of the features that distinguish human from animal consciousness.

Animals have rapid eye movement sleep—the same kind that is accompanied by dreaming in humans (see chapter 8). Do they dream? Although they can not tell us, it seems likely that they do have perceptual dream experience. Is it the same as ours? Do the dreams of animals have meaning? Do they play a role in the mental life of animals as they are thought to do in man? What, by the way, is the nature of "dream consciousness," and what is its relation to waking consciousness?

Having a dream is not unlike viewing a movie. The dreamer/viewer in each case experiences the action and emotions first-hand—as quite real in the case of the dream, in varying degrees with a movie, depending on how far one "gets into it." But there is one important difference: In the movie, the viewer takes what comes. The director controls what appears on the screen, and the

---

*Borrowed from Freud's metaphor to depict the relation of the "ego" to the "id" in governing the "instincts."

viewer, no matter how engaged, is basically passive, following where the screen leads. It may feel that way in a dream—"I wouldn't dream of such a thing," said the dreamer who had to be reminded that it was *his* dream. The director, producer, and all others involved in making movies utilize available stories, costumes, scenery, and sets. They choose the actors, actresses, and music. Not so with the dreamer, who supplies all of the above (substitute the word *emotion* for *music* here).

Where does the dreamer get all of the characters, props, and scripts for the dream? Obviously from within, from ideas and percepts that have been stored in memory somehow, somewhere in mind/brain. How do these percepts get into dream consciousness and what is the nature of the interrelationships among perceptions, memory, emotions, and consciousness and between waking and dream consciousness?

Often we take the most obvious things for granted. For example, considering the fact that we are constantly subjected to a veritable bombardment of sensory stimuli that have no intrinsic organization of their own, it is amazing that we experience the world and what is happening around us and to us as sensible, familiar, and understandable. We take it for granted that the world impinges upon our senses by presenting prepackaged and already categorized contents. Indeed, it does seem so to the adult but, as Gerald Edelman (1987) reminds us, it was not that way from the beginning for the newborn.

Think about a young animal in the wild. Before it can learn where the water hole is—and it will need to know that if it is not to spend an inordinate amount of time finding water by trial and error each time it is thirsty—it will first have to categorize the perceptual patterns that the water hole and its surrounds present to it. And not only will it have to find a way to distinguish and extract that pattern from any and all others it encounters, but it will somehow have to develop a way to retain information such as this for recall when needed. Without a way to categorize and retain such vital information, it might spend all its time and energy in the service of bare existence, and it will be unlikely to succeed in competition with animals that can do so. Is the memory of the water hole (and the path leading to it) stored as a veridical engram somewhere in the brain—something like a photographic negative waiting to be developed? That is unlikely; there do not seem to be enough neurons in the brain to do this. How then does it happen that an image is reexperienced in the "mind's eye" or in a dream? Or that a whole experience is remembered, even one that has long been forgotten?

But even though memories contain remembered sensations, images lose their sensory quality when they are consciously recalled during waking states. This, of course, is not true during the dreaming sleep state. As Freud points out in *The Interpretation of Dreams*:

> But if memories become conscious once more, they exhibit no sensory quality or a very slight one in comparison with perceptions. A most promising light would be thrown on the conditions governing the excitation of neurones if it could be confirmed that *in the ψ-systems memory and the quality that characterizes consciousness are mutually exclusive.* (Freud 1900, p. 540)

This quotation identifies a critical unanswered question: What is the relationship of memory to consciousness? Cognitive neuroscientists as well as psychoanalysts are interested in this and other, closely related mind/brain questions. It is becoming increasingly clear that psychoanalytic clinical data and experimental neurobiologic data often point in common directions. In regard to memory, contemporary data from both fields implicate emotion as the glue that binds memory elements to each other, enabling those that belong together to stay together. In the chapters that follow, we will trace separate lines of evidence from these seemingly disparate domains. Progress in these fields, particularly in cognitive neuroscience, is encouraging many scientists and scholars to take a fresh look and to seek closer approximations than have heretofore been possible. The search itself cannot but be exciting; along the way are myriad new facts to encounter and pregnant heuristic questions to contemplate, even before close integrations can (if ever) be expected to emerge.

PART I

CHALLENGING QUESTIONS

CHAPTER 1

Remembering and Forgetting in Dreaming Sleep

The Riddle of the Dream

A famous wise man was asked by two of his students to settle a heated argument about the meaning of a particularly obscure passage in a difficult text. After listening carefully to the first, he nodded in agreement: "You are right." After listening just as carefully to the second, he again nodded: "You, too, are right." A third student protested, "But their answers contradict each other. They can't *both* be right!" After careful reflection, the wise man answered, "Yes. You, too, are right."

"Dreams are for remembering. It's good to remember them." (right)

"Dreams are for forgetting. It's better to forget them." (right)

They can't both be right?

"I usually remember dreams when I wake up but forget them as the day goes on."

"I never remember my dreams no matter how hard I try. Maybe I don't dream at all."

"Sometimes I wake up remembering a vivid dream and can't get it out of my mind; it's unforgettable."

"There is one particular dream I've had many times."

"Sometimes I don't remember having dreamed when I wake up, but then a dream will come back to me while I'm in the shower, or while I'm driving to work."

"I woke up with a vivid dream Saturday morning and wrote it down so I could tell it to my analyst Monday. When I looked at my written notes on Monday, I didn't remember it at all. It was so strange that it could have been someone else's dream."

"Sometimes I remember a long-forgotten dream just after my analyst makes an interpretation."

All of the above reflect actual experiences. Will a single principle account for the inconsistencies? How are we to understand it all?

Freud was a "good dreamer." He was impressed with what he called the hypermnesis of dreams; on occasion he would encounter dream images that vividly reproduced sense impressions (perceptual residua) of objects or scenes that could only have been acquired during very early childhood experiences. Often these were experiences and images that had been long forgotten, and seeing them again was surprising, even startling. Many of his patients reported similar experiences. Most often the recollected childhood events had been emotionally charged, and frequently the actual objects and locations could be verified—identified and located in place and time.

Such experiences are by no means rare. Clearly, whether or not it is a good thing or a bad thing, it does happen that significant events, people, and objects can be remembered (even remembered with intense imagery) in dreaming sleep. Equally impressive is the opposite—the amount and degree of forgetting associated with dreams. Although most people usually have four or five (twenty-minute) periods of rapid eye movement (REM) sleep—the sleep state identified with dreaming—each night, most people do not remember dreams when they wake up; if they do, it is usually only the dreams from the last REM period of the night. Yet we can feel sure from laboratory studies that they did dream during each REM episode and would have reported dreams if they had been awakened during each of the REM periods.

Moreover, those dreams that are recalled in the morning are ordinarily forgotten before the day is over. To remember them often requires special attention or effort, and even then such efforts may not succeed. It doesn't seem on the face of it that dreams are intended, for the most part, to be remembered. Clearly, most of what we dream (approximately one to one-and-a-half hour's worth per night) is soon forgotten—a lot of forgetting!

It is clear that *both* remembering *and* forgetting occur in dreaming sleep. Here is a challenging paradox. Could it imply a special memory-processing role for REM sleep in adaptation/survival, its development as a special brain state, providing an important evolutionary advantage? After all, each of these opposite aspects of memory function is important for survival. The mind/brain simply cannot store all of the sensory input that impinges on it; to forget can be just as vital as to remember. As Francis Crick and Graeme Mitchison (1983) have pointed out, there would not be enough open neural circuits to register each new day's information—let alone store it—unless the circuits had been cleared to make room for it. Circuit clearing, they propose, is the role served each night by dreaming sleep. ("Dreams are for forgetting. It's better to forget them.")

But that particular argument may have been carried too far; it addresses only one side of the problem. The young forest creature (referred to in the general introduction) learning to find the water hole must both remember what is important (for example, particular landmarks on the way to the water or the den of a predator to be avoided) and forget what is unimportant (the myriad other irrelevant sense impressions it encounters along the way, such as leaves, shadows, and friendly creatures). For each individual sensory input, the critical question is whether to save it or discard it, and if it is to be saved, where to store it and how to do so in such a way that it can be retrieved when needed. What seems to be required is a computerlike data processing system to register, categorize, sort, store and file and retrieve information. The mind/brain does all of that, but of course much more.

A number of investigators (Palombo 1973, 1978; Greenberg and Pearlman 1974, 1975, 1980; Winson 1985) have suggested, each in different ways, that important memory processing, which must include both remembering and forgetting, is carried out during dreaming sleep. This is an intriguing idea, one that in principle seems to have face validity. It raises many of the provocative questions about mind/brain that motivate the inquiry to be presented in this book.

A DUAL-TRACK APPROACH

While, as mentioned earlier, it is reasonable to regard mind/brain as a single entity, its functions are manifest in two separate domains: one, the mental domain, deals with meanings and motives without physical properties, while the other, the biological domain, deals with matter and energy, which do display physical properties. In attempting to gain an empirically based understanding of this entity, we approach it by studying its observable manifestations, but these can be known only in terms of the separate sciences of mind and brain, which use different languages, observations, and concepts. This dichotomy places us in a dilemma. Observational units are not interchangeable between the domains; molecules are units of matter, not of behaviors or beliefs. Parallel—even simultaneous—observations of the same phenomena from the two vantage points at best produce only covariance data. Consequently, casual sequences cannot be assigned across domains.

One very reasonable way of dealing with this dilemma is first to approach the findings from each domain separately but in parallel, attempting to discern and develop principles of function that obtain in each realm. One can then compare and search for convergences—similarities, identities, or isomorphisms between principles and mechanisms that obtain in each of the two realms—and for obvious inconsistencies as well. Shared, isomorphic, or corresponding principles and clear inconsistencies should facilitate reconciliation of the two sets of data and alert scholars to indications for conceptual revisions on either or both sides.

In the chapters that follow, I propose just such a dual-track approach to the study of memory processes as they are manifested on the one hand in the mental content of dreams and, on the other hand, in physiologic events that occur during dreaming sleep in the brain structures and systems that are known to process perceptual input and to subserve information storage and retrieval.

While no means of translating between the two information modes is available, the two separate sets of information should be mutually complementary, rather than interchangeable (see also Lehtonen 1980, 1985). Both sets reflect different aspects of the processes under consideration and therefore should be helpful in addressing and broadening understanding of questions asked in this chapter and following chapters.

19

CHAPTER 2

Sense and Nonsense
in Dreams

To the sleeping dreamer, the dream experience seems real and in the present, despite the fact that it is not real and that the images and sensations of which the dream is composed actually were first registered during experiences that occurred before the dreams—often long before. The reason for the illusion is that during dreaming sleep, imagery is instigated by excitations of sensory cortex. The sleeper, not realizing that the excitatory stimuli are coming from within, cannot but interpret the images as real—that is, as if the stimuli were coming from outside, as they do during waking hours. Nor can the dreamer know that these internally generated stimuli are patterned after previous excitations and represent reactivations of perceptual residua stored from past experiences. Often the experiences themselves have been long out of mind, and the perceptual patterns have changed with time. These hallucinations occur regularly as part of normal dreaming sleep. (If they occurred during waking hours, they would be regarded as manifestations of mental disturbance.)

Indeed some of nature's most baffling mysteries, like those

posed by the dream, can be contained in experiences so common-place and familiar as to be overlooked. Here are mysteries aplenty. How and why does all this come about? What could possibly be the evolutionary value (if any) of such a process? Small wonder that there is confusion and disagreement about the nature of dreams, what they represent, and how they are to be explained!

One of the most important controversial issues concerns meaning in dreams. Do they convey meaning? If so, how? Could dream images be used and arranged in a special way for just such a purpose? There are serious students of the dream who assert that there is meaning in all dreams; others say there is meaning in none, or only in some, or some parts but not in others. Even among those who do attribute meaning to dreams, there is one very fundamental disagreement. Some consider it obvious and transparent; others regard it as "latent"—that is, hidden beneath the "manifest" content, censored and disguised for the deliberate purpose of conceal-ment. Indeed, some dreams do seem quite transparent, others bi-zarre and turgid. Could both views again be right, or partially so?

Many readers will already have recognized Freud's terminol-ogy and detected the "latent" controversy lurking under the simple ("manifest") statement of the question. Freud, as we all know, con-sidered meaning in dreams to be hidden by disguise and censor-ship. Some contemporary neurophysiological/psychiatric inves-tigators, on the other hand, hold the meaning to be transparent, with no censorship or disguise involved (see, for example, Hobson 1988 and Hobson and McCarley 1977).

The historical background of this controversy is important. Freud's theory of dreams was first published in 1900, at a time when there was relatively little known about the neurophysi-ology—let alone the psychophysiology—of dreaming sleep. Freud had already abandoned an early attempt to create a "Scientific Psychology" (Freud 1895). He gave it up because there was insuffi-cient knowledge about brain function to correlate with the richly complex observations of mental function that he was able to make using his psychoanalytic method of inquiry. From that time on he endeavored to construct instead a purely psychological theory of mind based exclusively on psychological observations. Nonetheless, he never abandoned his hope and belief that ultimately enough would be known to understand the workings of the mind in terms of the function of the brain.

It was not until after his death in 1939 that the amazing wealth of neurobiological information with which we are currently familiar became available. While it is true that he did not make major substantive revisions of his original dream theory, it is also true that there was little or no new neurobiological information about dreaming sleep that might have stimulated him to do so. REM sleep was first discovered in 1953.

Still, as pointed out by Amacher (1965) and more recently by Sulloway (1979) and others, Freud's psychologically cast theoretical formulations about mind do contain unmistakable echoes and imprints of physiological ideas and patterns of thought that had influenced his early attempt to construct a "Scientific Psychology," which he had abandoned and disavowed. This reflection should not be surprising; the knowledge of physiology in the nineteenth century, which was incomplete and incorrect in important respects, shaped the intellectual climate of the profession in which he had grown up, learned, lived, and worked. As background context, it must have influenced his thinking, even though he found it wanting and tried to make his theoretical formulations independent of it. How could it be otherwise?—same man, same brain, same mind. Indeed, this point does raise the question of whether aspects of psychoanalytic dream theory may have been flawed because of their context of origin. Any serious study of dreams such as this one must address this challenge and be prepared to entertain revisions.

The crux of the disagreement about meaning does not concern the empirical observations of dream phenomena themselves but rather their interpretation and theoretical elaboration. Therefore, in addressing the challenge, it is important to start by reviewing and evaluating a representative sample of Freud's primary data—

that is, his clinical observations and the immediate inferences he drew from them, which we will do in the next chapter. These data and data-close inferences—as well as current neurobiological data and inferences—should be taken into consideration in reevaluating abstract aspects of the theory.

There are some who would recommend discarding the rich observations and clinical insights detailed in *The Interpretation of Dreams* (Freud 1900) on the mistaken assumption that the historically based theoretical reservations mentioned above pertain to the primary clinical data as well. My opinion is quite to the contrary: Failure to take psychoanalytic clinical observations (and data-close inferences) into account will deprive the field of exactly the kind of psychological information required to achieve a balanced psychobiological model of dreams and dreaming sleep.

The study that follows focuses on one aspect of dreaming, its relation to memory, and the theoretical assertion that mnemic imagery may in fact be deployed in the dream to convey meaning. The purpose is not to debate or defend all of Freud's original dream text or to address the entire group of theoretical constructs commonly subsumed under the single designation of "psychoanalytic theory." For the reasons discussed above, psychoanalytic observations, inferences, and concepts concerning putative memory functions of the dream will be evaluated in light of contemporary neurobiologic and cognitive psychologic observations, inferences, and concepts. My hope is that this evaluation will lead to a point where some judgments can be made. Psychoanalytic concepts that no longer seem tenable in the light of the newer observations could then be regarded as dispensable. Equally important, those concepts that *do* still fit and continue, in competition with alternative explanations, to provide reasonable explanations of observed data could tentatively be retained. What, in other words, is the nature of the revisions that may be indicated, and how extensive need they be? Total? Partial? If partial, what parts?

This work started with a search for possible relationships between psychoanalytic and neurobiologic observations and concepts about memory processes in dreaming sleep. As it progressed, the search broadened to include cogent data from additional disciplines and extended to encompass relevant observations and concepts regarding emotion and regarding cognitive functions such as perception that also are intimately involved in dream process.

It happens that each of the four functions of mind/brain (memory, perception, emotion, and dreaming) are subjects of overlapping but separate interest to (and studies by) investigators from several different disciplines: psychoanalysis, cognitive psychology (including cognitive neuropsychology), and neurobiology (see figure 2.1). This circumstance provides an opportunity to compare and contrast independently derived data and concepts pertaining to phenomena of common interest to the various disciplines and to this study. Such an effort should be helpful in clarifying some issues, identifying cogent principles, and framing useful questions, even though it should be expected that definitive final answers will continue to be elusive for some time to come.

Several issues are for the most part agreed upon by investigators who work with human subjects, both patients and volunteer experimental subjects. First, meaning in dreams is ordinarily not apparent instantly, but some sense of it can emerge upon reflection—often quite promptly and easily. Second, dream accounts reflect the influence of mental work already done in the attempt to make sense of vague, strange, and bizarre aspects of the dream experience. These efforts can be likened to an editor's work in polishing a poorly organized rough draft and converting it into a credible narrative. Finally, the meanings that can be attached to dreams often turn out to be related to important conflicts and problems that are currently matters of concern to the dreamer. Often they have even been in the forefront of waking thoughts. Rosalind Cartwright's studies (1977) suggest that dreams of persons currently free of pressing emotional problems may be mundane and "uninteresting" in contrast to those of persons coping with serious life problems such as divorce.

The major questions are those that arise in connection with

FIGURE 2.1 Venn diagram depicting overlapping interests of neurobiology, psychoanalysis (PSA), and cognitive psychology (ψ) in memory, emotion, perception, and dreaming.

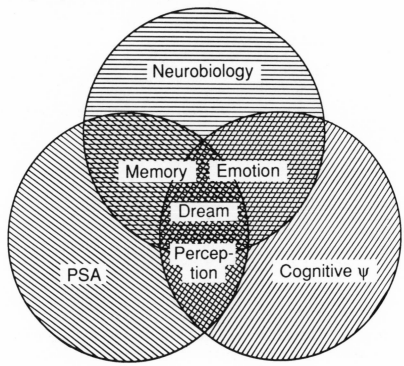

Freud's assertions about disguise and censorship. These assertions are based on observations and postulates that originated in the clinical situation and warrant evaluation in their own right. It should be borne in mind that the dreams of patients in psychoanalytic treatment may be different from those of subjects who volunteer for study in the sleep laboratory. Because psychoanalytic patients' dreams acquire special transference meanings and communication function, it is to be expected that these dreams may be richer in symbolic imagery and more productive of meaningful associations to that imagery.

FIGURE 2.2   Rebus

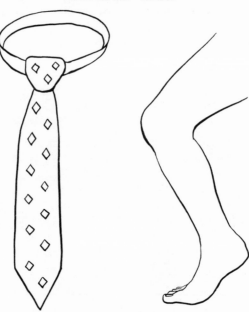

MEMORY AND MEANING IN FREUD'S DREAM THEORY:
A BRIEF INTRODUCTION

Freud noted that meaning may be carried by an image but that the meaning is not recognizable until the image is named—that is, until a verbal label is attached to it. As an illustrative example of this phenomenon, consider this rebus:

Viewing this rebus, one sees merely a picture of a tie and a knee drawn side by side. This picture does not, in and of itself, evoke any meaning beyond its intrinsic pictorial content. But the dual mental operation of first naming each of the drawn images and then combining the sounds of *tie* and *knee* to form the word *tiny* produces a word stimulus that *is* capable of evoking a recognizable meaning. Note that the connotative meaning of the word *tiny* goes beyond, and is not related to, the graphic content of the picture itself. In other words, under the proper conditions (that is, before this mental naming operation) the picture can stand for something other than itself. In this illustration the picture stands for a word that in turn connotes a meaning or idea; in other cases a picture could stand for another picture that then led to a word and in turn to an idea. (Some of the principles operating in image/word/meaning relationships, illustrated here by the rebus phenomenon, can also be observed in pantomime and in the game of charades.)

Freud had already observed that dreams are composed of sensory (mainly visual) images and that "free associations" evoked in the dreamer's mind by these images led to emotionally significant thoughts and memories. Taking these observations and the rebus phenomenon into account, he postulated that dream imagery could carry meanings in cognitively unrecognizable form and that dream images could be generated from "memory traces" of sensory stimuli that were originally registered during emotionally meaningful experiences. In other words, the dream could be regarded as a collage of mnemic perceptual images recruited and assembled in a way that would permit expression of hidden meanings.

These psychological postulates, which pertain only to the mental domain, occupy a central position in psychoanalytic dream theory and bear quite directly on the issue of disguised and concealed meaning in dreams. They are intimately related to actual phenomena Freud observed and described. They can and should be evaluated in the light of contemporary neurobiology and cognitive neuropsychology.

What better place to start than with the actual observations? Leaving more abstract theoretical issues for later (chapter 11), let us get on with the task and turn to a primary source: Freud's account of the dream of the botanical monograph in *The Interpretation of Dreams*.

PART II

MIND, PSYCHOANALYSIS: The First Key

CHAPTER 3

The Dream:
The Sleeping Mind at Work

If we adopt the method of interpreting dreams which I have indicated here, we shall find that dreams really have a meaning and are far from being the expression of a fragmentary activity of the brain, as the authorities have claimed. —(Freud 1900, p. 121)

While many of Freud's ideas and theories, like those in other sciences, are based on inferences that reach beyond immediate empirical data, the epigraph given here is of a different order. It follows quite directly from observations Freud was able to make using his method of free association—trains of images, ideas, and recollections that emerged unguided and uncensored as dreams were remembered and recounted.

The mind is active during dreaming sleep. As we shall shortly see, memory processes figure prominently in that activity—and memories often are intimately woven into the fabric of dreams. This being the case, it seems reasonable to expect that inquiry into the psychological nature of dreams should help in the search for principles by which memories are processed by the mind. This chapter will initiate that search. In later chapters, such psychologically derived mind principles as can be identified will be compared with neurobiologically derived brain principles by which memories are processed by the brain. We will then be in a position to look for patterns that seem to be—and may ultimately turn out to be—common to both domains.

In attempting to derive functional principles in a phenomenological domain, it is particularly important to deal first with observations themselves, insofar as possible considering them separately from theory. With this in mind, let us go back to a primary source and review a sample of Freud's raw data: the account of one of his most cogent dreams and his work with it. The purpose is to see what such a review can reveal about memory and mind in their own terms, in their own domain.

THE DREAM OF THE BOTANICAL MONOGRAPH

> I had written a monograph on a certain plant. The book lay before me and I was at the moment turning over a folded coloured plate. Bound up in each copy there was a dried specimen of the plant, as though it had been taken from a herbarium. (Freud 1900, p. 169)

I will follow Freud's text as he recounted his analysis of the dream. He began by reporting trains of thought that present in clusters or packages relating mainly to one or two words: *botanical* and *monograph*. A few relate to both and are regarded as intermediate. To illustrate, connections for many of the dream elements will be designated in parentheses in the text that follows (*B* = *botanical*, *M* = monograph).

For each train of thought, Freud also identified a connection in his mind to one of two incidents that took place the day preceding the dream. The first incident was seeing a book titled *The Genus Cyclamen* in a shop window, which became a part of the day's residue; the second was a long and emotionally meaningful conversation with Dr. Königstein "about a matter which never fails to excite my feelings whenever it is raised" (p. 171). Freud did not immediately specify the nature of that "matter." Later he mentions "blame for being too much absorbed in my favorite hobbies" (p. 173). He later alludes to the content of the conversation again without specifying details.

In order to convey as clearly as possible what I think can be discerned about memory from Freud's account, I will treat his account of his associations as a text to be analyzed. And my reading of it will be clinical—that is, in the mode of thinking and working ordinarily used in listening to and working with dreams in actual psychoanalytic practice.* Accordingly, it will be helpful first to take note of comments that identify an intensely important issue that was of great concern to him at the time of the dream and provided the background context of the conversation with Dr. Königstein. Ordinarily, the analyst's knowledge of the analysand's history and current problems provides a framework for organizing the account of the dream and the associations to it. Freud, being his own analyst, was courageous enough to suspend the usual need for personal privacy in order to provide his readers with relevant background information.

At the time of the dream, Freud was working on *The Interpretation of Dreams*. His most intense ambitions were centered on this book; on its completion, he was to write to his friend and confidant, Wilhelm Fliess:

> Do you suppose . . . that some day a marble tablet will be placed on the house, inscribed with these words?
>> "In This House, on July 24th, 1895
>> the Secret of Dreams was Revealed
>> to Dr. Sigm. Freud"?
>> (Freud 1900, p. 121)

*Readers are encouraged to consult the original text (Freud 1900, pp. 169–176 and 282–284) to gain their own firsthand impressions of it.

In 1884 Freud had written a dissertation on the coca plant that he felt had called Dr. Karl Koller's attention to the anesthetic properties of cocaine. He felt he might have been credited with the discovery, had he persisted in this line of endeavor—a near miss in the quest for fame.

FREUD'S ASSOCIATIONS TO THE BOTANICAL MONOGRAPH DREAM

In the discussion that follows, Freud's associations to the dream are illustrated in a series of diagrams constructed from his text. They are intended to depict schematically the associative connections that can be observed between the dream images and dream thoughts—first for the separate trains of thought (figures 3.1 to 3.5) and then for all of them together (figure 3.6).

Train 1

Freud began his account with a mention of seeing the book in the shop window. He noted that cyclamens were his wife's favorite flower *(B)*, which he frequently forgot to bring her, and then mentioned a successfully treated patient, Frau L., who provided an illustration (involving forgotten flowers) of his theory about forgetting. This train of thought clustered mainly around botanical topics and extended to the issue of attentiveness to his wife, to one of his theories, and to a patient who supported it (see figure 3.1).

Train 2

"I now made a fresh start" (p. 170). Freud recalled having written the dissertation on the coca plant *(B, M)*. This reminded him that

FIGURE 3.1 Train 1 in Freud's free associative trains of thought to the botanical monograph dream. In figures 3.1–3.5, nodal points (for example, favorite flowers, Königstein, cocaine) are ideas that connect with several others. Arrows indicate connections to nodes in other trains, indicating that each train is part of an overall nodal network.

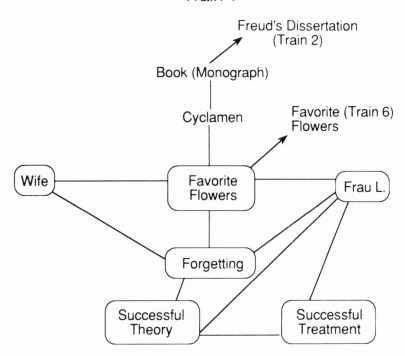

the morning after the dream, he had thought about the anesthetic properties of cocaine in a daydream, in which he fantasized that if he ever got glaucoma, he would consult an eye surgeon in a different city—incognito, in order to avoid awkwardness about billing. The surgeon, not knowing who he was, would boast of the ease of such operations since the introduction of cocaine.

Next Freud realized that a specific event was behind this fantasy: His father had been operated on for glaucoma by Dr. Königs-

FIGURE 3.2   Train 2 in Freud's associations to the botanical monograph
dream.

Train 2

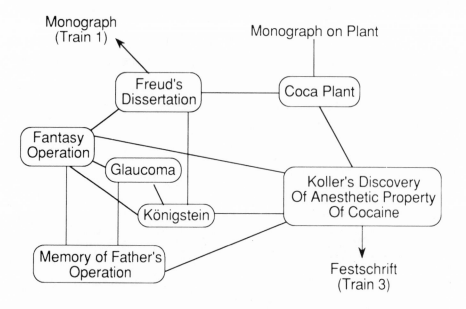

stein while Dr. Koller administered cocaine anesthetic. Koller had
mentioned that this brought together all three men who had been
involved in introducing cocaine (see figure 3.2). Another dream
relating to this same incident and centering on the same conflictual
issues is discussed on pages 39–40.

Train 3

Next came thoughts of a recent occasion that had reminded him of
cocaine. Looking at a copy of a *Festschrift* (*M*) in honor of the
leader of the laboratory where Koller had made his discovery,
Freud connected the dream in his mind with the walk with Dr.
Königstein and their conversation about a "matter that never fails

FIGURE 3.3   Train 3 in Freud's associations to the botanical monograph dream.

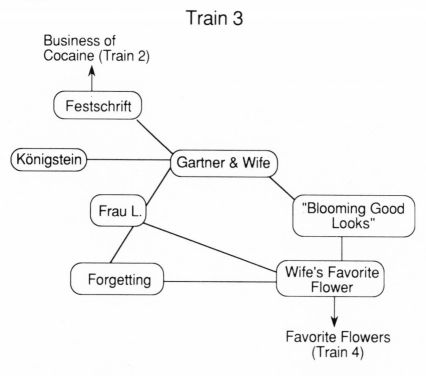

to excite my feelings" (p. 171). It had been interrupted by the arrival of Dr. Gartner ("Gardener"—*B*). Freud had congratulated him and his wife on their "blooming" (*B*) good looks. Freud's patient Flora (*B*) was mentioned. Dr. Gartner was another author represented in the *Festschrift* (*M*), and Frau L. (*B*) had also been mentioned (see figure 3.3).

Train 4

Freud then turned his attention to the dried specimen of the plant (*B*) in the dream. The monograph (*M*) looked like a herbarium (*B*), which brought to mind a memory of an incident that had occurred when he was in secondary school. (Note that while the previous memories connected with the dream were all relatively recent ones, this one went back farther in time, to what may be called the intermediate past.) The headmaster gave pupils the school's herbarium (*B*) to clean. There were bookworms in it. Freud was given a sheet including Cruciferae (*B*). He was also given a crucifer to identify in his preliminary examination in botany, and he failed to identify it correctly. *Cruciferae* brought to mind *Compositae* (*B*), which include artichokes—his favorite flowers—which his wife does not forget to bring home for him (see figure 3.4).

Train 5

In the dream, he saw the monograph lying open before him. In a letter Freud had received the day before the dream, Fliess had written that he could visualize Freud's dream book finished: "I see it lying before me and I see myself turning over its pages" (*M*; p. 172).

Train 6

The folded colored plate brought to mind his strong preference while in medical school for studying from monographs (*M*) and his special attraction to their colored plates. Somehow this brought up a memory from the distant past. When he was five years old, his father gave him and his sister a book to destroy. With pleasure he remembered the two of them pulling the pages with colored plates apart "leaf by leaf like an artichoke" (*M, B*). Later, as a medical student, his passion for owning books was a favorite hobby, and he had become a bookworm. His book-buying led him into debt and incurred his father's disapproval. This thought reminded him again

FIGURE 3.4   Train 4 in Freud's associations to the botanical monograph dream.

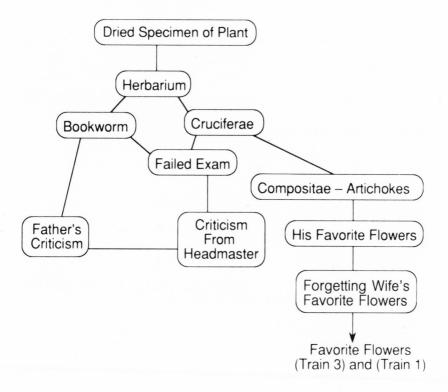

Train 4

of his conversation with Dr. Königstein, "for in the course of it we had discussed the same question of my being blamed for being too absorbed in my *favourite hobbies*" (p. 173; see figure 3.5).

In a later dream about Count Thur (Freud 1900, p. 209), to which he did not refer in discussing this one, Freud handed a male glass urinal to an old man who was blind in one eye. In his discussion of this latter dream Freud stated that the old man "clearly was my father, since his blindness in one eye referred to his unilateral

FIGURE 3.5   Train 6 in Freud's associations to the botanical monograph dream.

Train 6

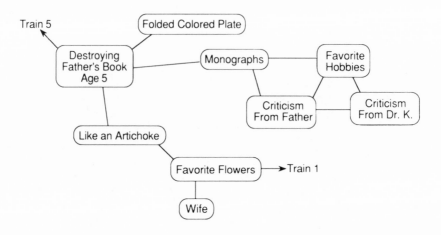

glaucoma" (p. 216). In connection with this dream, he recalled an incident from age seven or eight years of age, when he

> disregarded the rules which modesty lays down and obeyed the calls of nature in my parents' bedroom while they were present. In the course of his reprimand, my father let fall the words: "The boy will come to nothing." This must have been a frightful blow to my ambition, for references to this scene are still constantly recurring in my dreams and are always linked with an enumeration of my achievements and successes, as though I wanted to say: "You see, I *have* come to something."   (Freud 1900, p. 216)

I mention this here to introduce the idea that this dream and memory are linked to the botanical monograph dream through repetition of common thought elements and reference to common feelings. The significance of this observation will be discussed later in this chapter.

FREUD'S INTERPRETATION OF THE BOTANICAL
MONOGRAPH DREAM

Freud's interpretive comments begin with the following observation:

> All the trains of thought starting from the dream—the thoughts about my wife's and my own favourite flowers, about cocaine, about the awkwardness of medical treatment among colleagues, about my preference for studying monographs and about my neglect of certain branches of science such as botany—all of these trains of thought, when they were further pursued, led ultimately to one or other of the many ramifications of my conversation with Dr. Königstein.
>
> (p. 173)

And he noted that these thoughts, like those expressed by his earlier dream of Irma's injection (pp. 107–121), seem to have been "in the nature of a self-justification. . . . What it [the form of the dream] meant was 'After all, I'm the man who wrote the valuable and memorable paper (on cocaine)' " (p. 173). He took this to mean that the dream thoughts had been dominated by the very same concerns that had occupied him during the day; in this sense, the dream did indeed have meaning.

Freud interpreted the fact that the manifest content of the dream referred to a relatively indifferent event (day's residue) as meaning that the image registered during the indifferent event had served in the dream as an allusion to a second, highly meaningful event. The associational links were revealed in the intermediate bridging ideas, such as those connected to Dr. Gartner and his participation in the *Festschrift*, which in turn referred to cocaine and the associations with it. Then, after listing many of the main associations that clustered around the word *botanical* (Dr. Gartner, blooming looks, patients Flora and Frau L., favorite flowers, the secondary school incident with the herbarium and the examina-

41

tion, his favorite hobbies, the scene from his childhood), he made a striking observation:

> Thus "botanical" was a regular nodal point in the dream. Numerous trains of thought converged upon it. . . . So, too, "monograph" in the dream touches upon two subjects: the one-sidedness of my studies and the costliness of my favourite hobbies. (p. 283)

Each of the words, *botanical* and *monograph*, was connected to multiple underlying dream thoughts that converged on and imparted multiple meanings to it: "each of the elements of the dream's content turns out to have been 'overdetermined'—to have been represented in the dream-thoughts many times over" (p. 283).

Thus did Freud describe the relationship between the manifest and the latent content of the dream. Later he would invoke the still-controversial concept of psychic energy and use the terms *condensation* and *displacement* (which are descriptive of the phenomenon of overdetermination referred to above) to label the hypothetical mental mechanisms that he constructed to explain the observations. But the observations themselves stand as real, whether or not the hypothetical constructs ultimately turn out to be valid.

Figures 3.1 through 3.6, which were constructed from Freud's text, are intended schematically to depict the associative connections that can be observed to obtain between the dream images and dream thoughts—first for each of the trains of thought separately (3.1-3.5), and then for all of them together (3.6). As these diagrams illustrate, following Freud's concept of "nodal points," the dream images and underlying thoughts can be viewed as organized in a nodal network pattern (see Figure 3.6). As a matter of fact, in addition to what might be termed the major nodes—that is, those that Freud identified (*botanical* and *monograph*)—each of the trains of thought or sectors of the larger network can be seen to display elements within it that have multiple connections and

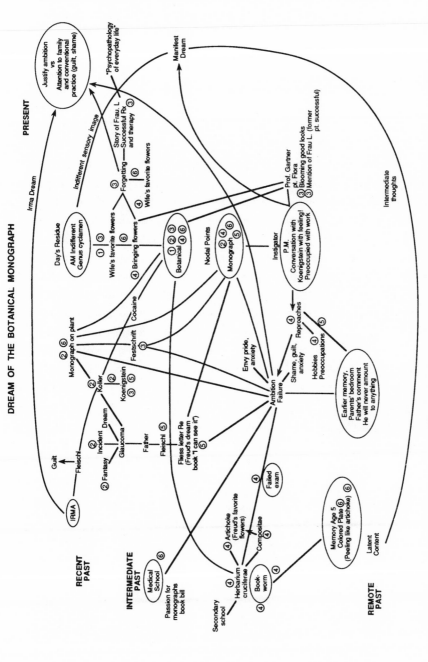

FIGURE 3.6 The nodal memory network underlying Freud's dream of the botanical monograph. The circled numbers refer to the trains of thought in which the thoughts were expressed. Historical location of memories is roughly depicted by a counterclockwise scheme starting with the present time in the upper righthand corner.

might be regarded as minor or subnodes: for example, "favorite flowers" in trains 1, 3, 4, and 6, Königstein in train 2, and Dr. Gartner and his wife in train 3.

IMPLICATIONS OF THE DREAM FOR MEMORY

If the dream image of the botanical monograph was indeed borrowed from the perceptual experience of the morning and reproduced in the dream for the purpose of serving as an allusion to the emotionally charged conversation with Dr. Königstein, how might this process have come about? To venture an answer will take us beyond the data and into the realm of inference and speculation.

In his account, Freud makes it clear that at the time of these events, he was preoccupied with worries about the fact that intensely ambitious professional strivings were creating conflicts in his personal and professional life. He recognized that these problems were activated during his conversation with Dr. Königstein; all associative trains of thought led to it.

> The second experience had a high degree of psychical importance: I had a good hour's lively conversation with my friend the eye-surgeon; in the course of it I had given him some information which was bound to affect both of us closely, and I had had memories stirred up in me which had drawn my attention to a great variety of stresses in my own mind. . . . A further set of connections was then established—those surrounding the idea of cocaine, which had every right to serve as a link between the figure of Dr. Königstein and a botanical monograph which I had written. . . .   (1900, pp. 174–176)

Somehow the actual image of the book that he had noticed in the shop window was transformed into the image of the book in the dream. The key changes from the actual image of the book to the dream image of the book are few and modest. They concern added details: "turning over a folded coloured plate . . . a dried specimen of the plant, as though . . . from a herbarium" (p. 169).

Taken along with other dream elements (plant, monograph, "the book which lay before me"), these few images and elements evoke memories of quite a large number of associated images and thoughts. Although the evoked images and thoughts are numerous, the emotional issues embedded in them can be regarded as an organized unit, a composite of two clusters of feelings, each tightly bound to one or the other side of the polarity of *ambition* and *failure*. One feeling cluster (envy, pride, and anxiety) belongs to *monograph* and centers on ambition. For example:

one dream image
Monograph on a certain plant→
coca plant→
Koller's discovery of its anesthetic properties→
fantasy operation→
memory of Father's actual operation→
Königstein (many thoughts)→
ambition, envy, pride, anxiety
one feeling cluster

The other feeling cluster (guilt, shame, and anxiety) belongs to *botanical* and centers on failure. Each train of thought with its multiple images, ideas, and memories leads to one or the other pole of the emotional complex, and some lead to both (see figure 3.7).

DERIVING A PRINCIPLE OF MEMORY ORGANIZATION: A FIRST APPROXIMATION

The disproportions between the small number of image elements in the dream, the large number and variety of associative images and thoughts, and the small, tightly organized cluster of feelings may provide a clue to an organizing principle of memory and

FIGURE 3.7 The connections between the individual trains of thought and the affective polarities of ambition and failure.

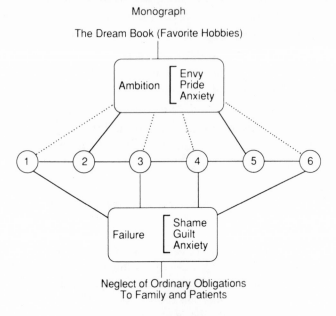

Monograph

The Dream Book (Favorite Hobbies)

Neglect of Ordinary Obligations
To Family and Patients

Botanical

dream construction. (Bear in mind that it is principles that we are seeking in this endeavor.) It could be that affect is the factor that connects dream images to memories. More specifically, dream images and the memory traces they represent may be associatively linked by a capacity to evoke the same emotions. And the observed overdetermination of dream images and thoughts (one image standing for numerous thoughts, and one thought represented by numerous images) would suggest that nodal images and thoughts would be those with a capacity for linkage with perceptual residua of experiences carrying the same affective potential, as illustrated in figure 3.8.

The term *affect* is used here as synonymous with emotion and

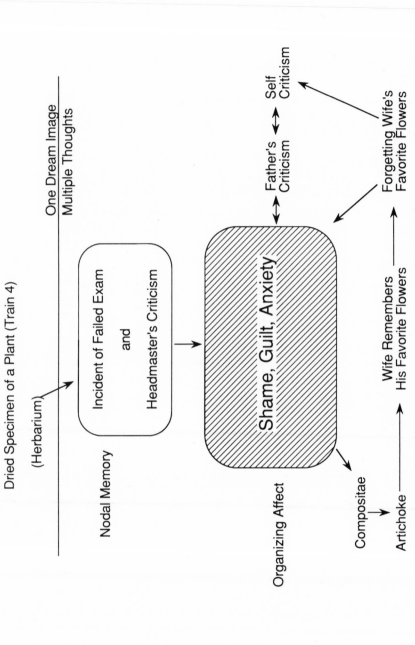

FIGURE 3.8 A single dream image (dried specimen of a plant) and the multiple ideas represented in the associations to it. The diagram illustrates the putative role of the affect cluster, evoked by the idea of failure, in organizing mnemic perceptual images and ideas as a network.

is considered to consist of three components: motor, sensory, and subjective. The motor component consists of objective bodily changes that reflect neuroendocrine activation—for example, changes in heart rate and respiration. The sensory component consists of the bodily sensations that result from being made aware of those objective changes in the body, via visceroceptive sensory nerves. The subjective or feeling tone component consists of a private inner sense, such as apprehension, gloom, or sense of impending death or disaster.

Following Freud's usage (1900), I will consider affective states to be "all or nothing" phenomena. Awake or asleep, they are either present or absent. In this strict sense, affect, consisting in part of a bodily motor discharge, cannot be repressed in the same way that thoughts and ideas can. In this same sense it is incorrect to speak of repressed emotion; instead, one can speak of *potential affect* or *affective potential* in the same way as one can speak of energy as *kinetic* (active) or *latent* (potential). (For example, the kinetic or active energy of a falling object is absent before it is dropped, but it is latent or potential. The term *repressed emotion,* when used in a clinical context, is thus really a shorthand way of saying that a conflictual idea that *could* generate an active emotion has been detached from consciousness by repression and replaced by a substitute idea that can represent it without being recognized for what it really is. When the conflictual idea is disguised in this way, its affect is only potential.

Within such a conceptual framework, an individual manifest dream image can be regarded as a highly condensed referent, like a symbol in a code or software program, whereby the dream image can give access to an entire network of stored memories that are related to each other by shared affective potential. In other words, I am suggesting several things: first, that an emotionally charged experience can be represented by sensory information, percepts that were registered during that experience; second, that memories of many experiences involving the same emotions (and accordingly

48

carrying the same affective potential) could be represented by an image connected with one of them—a "nodal image"—through the process that Freud called condensation; and finally, that a nodal image, in addition to organizing a network of memory-related images around it, could also link to and activate nodal images in other networks originating in and representing life experiences from other contexts that involved the same affect or affects and thereby carry the same affective potential.

This is a fanciful metaphor indeed but, all the same, one that is consonant with the observed data, albeit from a single dream. Note that those ideas which can be inferred directly from the observations that we have reviewed in this chapter account for the fact that deeper latent meanings can be derived by association from the manifest content of the dream. Such a description does not invoke a censor or ascribe purpose to the fact that ideas may thus be indirectly expressed but not recognized during dreaming sleep. That is another matter, to be discussed in chapter 11, after we've covered much more ground.

Although the idea of memories being organized in nodal networks arose from study of this single dream, there are implications that the basic elements and structure of the network exposed by the dream may actually have been in place before—and might survive after—the occurrence of the dream itself. I think it is quite reasonable to regard networks revealed by a single dream as part of a more extensive and enduring organized system of memories that could be exposed by a longitudinal study of the dreamer.

First, the section of Freud's text about this dream refers to another, earlier dream, the "Irma" dream (see figure 3.6). Freud noted that the earlier dream dealt with the same conflictual issue of ambition and failure and that in it he tried to resolve the issue by asserting a similiar self-justification. The manifest element in that dream—"a white patch and turbinal bones with scabs on them" (p. 111)—referred in his associations to cocaine and thence to serious reproaches that had been directed to him, and to self-reproaches as well. The idea of cocaine and related images served as a major node in both the botanical monograph and the Irma dreams. Thus, as a common, highly charged element, it provided a link between the two dreams and the nexi of ideas and memories underlying each of them.

The same "cocaine node," along with reference to the ambition/failure issue, also appears in the later dream about Count Thur (Freud 1900, p. 208, 216), mentioned earlier in this chapter. In this instance, as in the Irma dream, associations led to some of the same—as well as to different—ideas and memories. And as might be expected, in view of the fact that *The Interpretation of Dreams* chronicled many of the dreams of Freud's self-analysis, this centrally important problem is encountered recurrently in the book via a variety of associative paths and nodes other than cocaine, which figures so prominently in these three dreams.

THE NODAL MEMORY NETWORK—A FIRST POSTULATE

What begins to emerge, then, is the idea of extended and enduring networks of mental representations. According to such a postulate, analysis of individual dreams reveals parts of the extended network, and portions of the individual networks of different dreams connect with one another when the ideas they represent are connected by common affective threads that lead to shared nodes (see figure 3.6). And when a sufficient number of connections can be traced by longitudinal study, there will emerge an overall pattern of affective themes carrying perceptual memory traces from progressively earlier and earlier life experiences and converging on core unresolved conflictual issues such as the one about ambition and failure in Freud's botanical monograph dream. Recall from figure 3.7 that all six trains of thought are interconnected; for example, following the connections depicted in figures 3.1 to 3.5, one can see that all trains except 2 and 5 connect directly to the "failure" pole through Freud's wife's favorite flowers (B), which in turn connects them through Königstein to 2, which links it to the "ambition" pole via 2 and 6, and thence indirectly back to 5 (M), and so on. (Interested readers can trace out the myriad redundant interconnections via the condensed nodal elements of the network.)

I have reviewed the empirical data in Freud's original text in great detail because these are the data that led him to the idea of nodal points in the content of dreams. And by extending the review to include further observations gleaned from others of Freud's dreams discussed in the same volume, I have suggested extending the concept to include the idea that nodal memory networks, so conceived, may be durable over time. Does such an idea hold up in the light of clinical experience with other patients? It does indeed.

As a matter of fact, the stimulus for this study arose the other way around. The idea of returning to Freud's text and examining it in this particular way followed from clinical experience with my patients. Repeatedly, in individual patients, I would encounter certain ideas and images that recurred very frequently in dreams and associations, especially during "good hours"—therapy sessions when significant new memories appeared, often accompanied by new insights. Somehow these experiences brought to mind the nodal points discussed in the botanical monograph dream and suggested that the recurrent images and ideas may have appeared in "good hours" precisely because they were nodal points.

Moreover, these nodal points could be expected to lead into significant associative trains that would bring us centripetally closer to earlier memories, centrally important unresolved conflicts, and traumatic life experiences. The idea seemed clinically useful. When such an image or idea appeared, calling it to the patient's attention and encouraging associations to it would often lead into productive new paths for the analytic work.

A previously reported study of a completed analysis—the case of Carol (Reiser 1984)—illustrated this principle in great detail. In that instance it was possible to discern and schematically diagram an enduring nodal memory network and to trace its associative pathways inward to a truly cataclysmic early life experience, the mother's death in childbirth when the analysand was four and a half years old. That experience had given rise to unresolved conflicts and major symptoms, including a major hysterical dissociative episode, with amnesia for a detail of it that persisted until, twenty-five years later, the detail was finally recovered through analysis of a dream; a hysterical abdominal pain syndrome, resolved by analytic work with a series of dreams; a subway phobia, also resolved by analytic work in which dreams played a large role; and a number of longstanding neurotic character traits, including an inability up to the age of thirty-four to fall in love and marry—also rooted in the nuclear cataclysmic experiences which began with the death of her mother. One of the major sources of her inability to fall in love and marry was rooted in a conviction that she would be certain to die in childbirth, as her mother had died, were she to marry and become pregnant. The case will be discussed in greater detail in chapter 5.

The principle underlying the phenomenon of nodal memory networks organized by affective links has been easily discernible in many cases, not only in my experience but in that of colleagues who have been alerted to it. It was these repeated clinical experiences that stimulated me to go back to the original text of "The Dream of the Botanical Monograph." As we have seen, Freud's original text turns out not only to illustrate the nodal concept in more vivid detail than he provided, but also to support the additional idea of durability (which may very well have been in his mind, although he did not make it explicit).

The capacity of the psychoanalytic method to generate data and to discern principles concerning memory processes in the mental domain is thus quite clear; this point will be further illustrated and amplified in chapter 5. The use of psychoanalytic process as a method of inquiry is not without its problems, however. Psychoanalysis as a method of research is inseparable from psychoanalysis as therapy, if for no other reason than that people are not willing to undergo the rigors and discomfort of the procedure in the absence of motivation generated by clinical distress, and without hope of relieving that distress through understanding. Herein lie both the strength and the weakness of the process as a research tool. No other method of inquiry gives access to the same depth and kind of information regarding human experience, but the method does not yield to the ordinarily more rigorous technical, methodological, and design demands of more conventional "hard sciences."

Because clinical psychoanalysis does provide unique entry to phenomena of great interest, the methodological problem of dealing with the data represents a serious challenge. The next chapter will examine the nature of psychoanalytic clinical data—its potential strength as well as its limitations—and compare it with the nature of neurobiologic data, alongside which it is later to be examined. In the course of this inquiry new and important ideas emerge concerning the role of the analyst's memory in psychoanalytic process. As will be seen in chapter 5, these ideas carry clinical as well as research implications.

CHAPTER 4

A Serious
Methodological Challenge

Before turning to further clinical psychoanalytic data, it would be well to confront important differences in the nature of observations in the two domains of brain and mind, and hence differences in the nature and credibility of postulated functional principles that can be inferred in each of them. These differences could turn out to be a serious matter for this study, for it is the inferred functional principles that I propose to compare, assuming that the search for similarities between postulated mind principles and postulated brain principles reveals ways in which their respective concepts may be converging. Such convergences should—in addition to their intrinsic intellectual interest—have heuristic value as well. For example, they might suggest questions of mutual or reciprocal interest to investigators in both fields and generate collaborative basic or clinical research.

If differences in the nature of the observations themselves are not recognized and taken into account, however, the comparisons may be inappropriate and the conclusions erroneous. It would be as though we were to search for principles governing fruit color by comparing the ultrastructure of apple skin with the mineral content of orange rind. The phenomenon of a monkey in the laboratory remembering which of two objects was present a few minutes earlier is not comparable to the phenomenon of a patient on the analytic couch remembering with vivid recall and strong feelings a long-forgotten, complex life event. Accordingly, before proceeding further into the study itself, let us look more closely into the nature of each of the two sets of observations, identify their important differences, determine which differences will constitute liabilities and which will represent assets in the proposed study, and specify areas where the psychoanalytic method can be expected to yield data appropriate for study alongside cognitive neuroscientific data about memory processes in the brain.

NEUROSCIENTIFIC DATA AND PSYCHOLOGICAL DATA

Investigators in the biological sciences work for the most part with phenomena that manifest themselves in the physical realm of matter and energy. Such phenomena can be detected by sensing instruments that record, measure, and otherwise define biological events as objectively as available technology permits, without distortion by personal observer bias. The same holds true for almost all cognitive neuroscience research, which is anchored primarily in brain science and uses behavioral paradigms in its experiments on animals and man. To the degree that objectifying data is possible—and it is quite high in the brain sciences—reliability and reproducibility can be established. These are critical criteria in the canons of empirical science; we are all aware of the high degree of scientific credibility with which such data and related data-close inferences are justifiably endowed. (Less justifiably, speculations more removed from the data may sometimes enjoy comparably high degrees of social respectability, interest, and acceptance through a halo effect.)

How very different it is with the mind studied by the psycho-analytic method. In this case ideation—a central phenomenon under study—is manifested in the realm of meaning. But meanings have no observable or measurable manifestations in the physical realm. They are accessible to introspection, communicated in language and other expressive media, and understood by inference, empathy, and intuition. In psychoanalysis, meanings—which are after all central objects of study—are inextricably embedded in private interpersonal interchanges. The basic data upon which inferences, hypotheses, and theory are based are extracted from the *memory* of one of the two participants, namely the analyst, who is both participant observer and reporter. Thus the primary recording instrument is the analyst's mental apparatus. It selectively detects, records, remembers or forgets, evaluates, and reports.

In other words, the analyst's record is not a veridical record of the session, nor can it be regarded as reflecting directly (or only) the analysand's mental processes, in the same way that an electro-encephalographic tracing can be regarded as a manifestation of underlying physiological brain processes in a patient. The analyst's reported account cannot be consensually validated, and therefore its reliability cannot be established.

Understandably, this limitation has cast doubt on the scientific credibility of psychoanalytic theory. Researchers have made serious efforts to overcome this problem by making audio or audio-visual recordings of psychoanalytic treatments and submitting them to independent study by several observers. Manuals have been devised for scoring transcripts of treatment sessions, and reliability has been established for many of the scales, even for a few that rate quite complex inferences, such as specifically defined qualities of transference phenomena. In some studies, simultaneous physiologic recordings have also been made and studied for correlations with concomitant psychologic events observed in the tapes. A large and continually growing literature documents the power of this approach (Dahl et al. 1978; Gill and Hoffman 1981;

Horowitz 1979; Knapp, Mushatt, and Nemetz 1966; Knapp et al. 1970; Luborsky 1973, 1976, 1984; Luborsky et al. 1979; Weiss and Sampson 1986). The fact that tape recording is now so well established as an experimental method—and the fact that methods for evaluating and scoring the tape records are continually being upgraded—represents a giant step forward in dealing with the reliability aspect of the observational data problem.

THE DUALITY IN PSYCHOANALYTIC DATA

There is another aspect of such data that warrants attention and serious study. Exactly what does a record of an analytic session actually reflect, regardless of whether it is the analyst's account or a tape recording? Consider that an analytic session is a process in which the mental activities of the analyst interact with those of the patient, and that in constructing a report, the analyst's mental processes are interposed between those of the patient and the text of the report. To write the report, the analyst must draw upon a memory that is a composite of not only the patient's reported thoughts, feelings, and memories but also the analyst's comments, thoughts, feelings, and memories.

Several years ago Donald Ross and Fred Kapp (1962) noted instances of fantasies or images drifting into the analyst's mind during a session. At first these mental intrusions seemed to be extraneous and irrelevant to the analytic work, but upon reflection, they could be clearly identified as thematically and affectively related to issues the patient was working with during that hour. Paying attention to them often helped to identify issues or aspects of the material that had escaped the analyst's notice up to that point.

Both Theodore Jacobs (1975) and James McLaughlin (1987) have provided extensive data richly documenting the finding that careful study of nonverbal motoric and postural phenomena and of imagery and fantasy, in both analyst and patient, can be of immense value in identifying and understanding important aspects of the analytic process—particularly those concerning transference, countertransference, and empathy. Both authors emphasize the importance of attending to these phenomena in everyday clinical psychoanalytic work. The Committee on Scientific Activities of the American Psychoanalytic Association is currently working on a proposed format for clinical reports that would include notes concerning the analyst's thoughts and feelings in parallel with the report of what patient and analyst said (Shane and Klumpner 1989).

In short, records that reveal only the patient's part cannot reflect the full interaction, especially the way events occurring in the memory system of the analyst may have influenced cognitive processes in the patient. What the analyst thought, felt, and remembered during the session does not leave a physical trace on the tape recording, yet it is important information. Moreover, the memory of the analyst contains more than the product of the intrinsic workings of the patient's mind; it includes a record of two minds working together. A large part of that record can be retrieved in consciousness and studied as a text in its own right. This, I submit, constitutes a special opportunity. It is a unique asset that the psychoanalytic method can bring to research on memory.

AN ANSWERING POSTULATE:
INTERACTING MEMORY NETWORKS IN
PSYCHOANALYTIC PROCESS

With such a text as a source of data, we can begin to postulate how the memory systems of analyst and analysand interact reciprocally in the psychoanalytic process. The postulate under development is derived from, and is intended to extend, the concept of the enduring nodal memory network (Reiser 1984; see also chapter 3). It can be stated in preliminary form as follows:

As the analytic process proceeds, there is encoded in the analyst's memory a version (analyst's version, AV) of the patient's nodal memory network (patient's version, PV), which the analyst has derived from what the patient has communicated. As the work progresses and the patient tells more of the history, more of it is encoded in the analyst's memory, and the overlap or shared portion increases. When a particular segment of the shared portion is active in one (for example, in PV), there will be an increased probability for the corresponding segment to be activated in the other (in this case, AV). In this way the analyst, by following the flow of the patient's thoughts, can respond with references to relevant historical material, appropriately phrased. Such communication between the two memory systems clinically manifested as empathy would be mediated or facilitated by overlapping affective tone.

This is a retrospectively derived postulate, which is based on clinical observations and experiences that will be described in detail in the next chapter in order to enable readers to share in them and to follow the reasoning involved in developing ideas from and about them. The clinical accounts will provide "work samples" to demonstrate the generative power of the psychoanalytic process for developing a new and heuristically promising postulates by investigating aspects of mental function that are not accessible by other, nonintrospective methods. The nature of this aspect of psychoanalytic process and its generative capacity can be explicated by tracing the way in which this postulate emerged from the clinical experiences.

TRACING THE DEVELOPMENT OF THE POSTULATE
(A NATURALISTIC STUDY)

As we saw in chapter 3, the story begins with the concept of the enduring nodal memory network, which was developed from the earlier study of the case of Carol (Reiser 1984) and from Freud's account of the dream of the botanical monograph (1900). In the course of the earlier clinical study, several questions were raised concerning the memory of the analyst. They arose in connection with two incidents in which something that I remembered from the patient's history seemed to release highly significant, previously repressed memories in the patient. The questions were:

> What is the nature of the processes that clued my memory system to the importance of the dream's issue of not being able to remember a name, and linked it *in my mind* to the story of the tapioca incident that I had heard four years previously? (Reiser 1984, p. 44)

> Why did I remember the dream first and then the actual event of the visit to the cemetery? Can study of a "dialogue" such as this between the memory systems of analyst and analysand provide any heuristic hints about memory storage, coding, and recall . . . ?
> (Reiser 1984, p. 47)

The present study begins with these questions—the ones with which the earlier study ended.

Step 1

The investigation of memory networks was extended to include the analyst as well as the patient and the possible interactions between the two networks. This process entailed review of the original case record with the aim of identifying and understanding instances in which my memory processes seemed to have been meaningfully involved in the analytic process—that is, instances in which memories came unbidden into my mind during analytic sessions or later after the treatment had been terminated and could be connected with significant memories in the patient's mind.

Several additional instances beyond those noted in the original report were identified. They, as well as additional reflections on such instances, are detailed in the next chapter. The recovered memories included experiences from my own personal life as well as experiences from Carol's life that she had told me about in previous hours.

Step 2

The next undertaking was the review of Freud's text on the dream of the botanical monograph (1900) and further clarification of the concept of the enduring nodal memory network.

Step 3

Having been alerted to phenomena of this nature, I was sensitized in subsequent analytic work to listen for evidence of such interchanges during analytic hours. Work with two patients furnished examples, to be reported in chapter 5. First, an incident in the analysis of a young man (Richard) alerted me to an additional dimension of these memory interactions. In that instance, a personal—temporarily unrecognized—reminiscence in me induced a mood that sensitized me to a detail of his dream. Inquiry into that particular aspect of the dream imagery led to recovery of significant new history from the patient—history strikingly consonant with the emotional content of my troubled reminiscence. That new historical material deepened our understanding of an important epoch of his life. The second incident, involving a young woman

(Eve), illustrates a similiar but much more complicated and extended interaction. In this instance my personal recollection, in the form of a vivid image in my "mind's eye," seemed clearly to have been activated by an empathic response to what she was telling me. Subsequently it exerted a powerful influence on the further development of the analytic process.

Interestingly, it was possible to relate all three interactions to a personal memory/affect network in my mind; since it reveals only that I loved my mother, I will have no difficulty divulging it. Nodal memories in that network could in each instance be seen to connect and interact with memory nodes in the patients that involved their own versions of the same or very similar affects.

Again the linkage of affect and memory move onto center stage: reciprocal interactions between the memory systems of analyst and analysand appear to be mediated by affect, to be related to empathy, and to play a meaningful role in the analytic process. Note that these ideas derive from psychological observations in the realm of the mind. As we will see in chapter 7, the physiological systems mediating affect in the biological realm are intimately involved in encoding sensory percepts into neural memory systems (in the realm of the brain). In both domains, the derived functional principles (the principles that are ultimately to be compared) are presumed to operate in networks—nodal memory networks in the mind, neural networks in the brain. Will similarities between principles in the two domains (for example, the mediating role of emotion) suggest actual conceptual convergence rather than mere semantic resemblance?

As will be seen in chapter 11, the mediating role of affect in associatively linking sensory percepts can be hypothesized to play a role in the construction of the dream, by organizing perceptual residua for appearance as images in dream consciousness during REM sleep. This is a bridging concept, pointing to convergence of separately derived functional principles from each of the two domains, principles that would appear to pertain to the same phenomenon—or at least to similar or parallel phenomena—observed in two different ways.

But I have skipped many intermediate steps and gotten far ahead of the story. I did so out of a conviction that both the nature of the data from the mental realm *and* the direction in which the argument is heading should be kept in mind as the clinical data are reviewed. The bridging concept cited above depends for its credibility on whether or not the functional principles derived from the observational data of the two realms, obtained by different methods, are indeed comparable.

CHAPTER 5

Memory and Dreams in Clinical Psychoanalytic Process

The Role of the Analyst's Memory

This chapter reviews the clinical experiences that gave rise to the ideas and postulates discussed in preceding chapters. It culminates in a detailed exposition of the book's central psychoanalytic hypothesis and an assertion of the special role of affect in organizing memories in the mind. Although the observations do not lend themselves to conventional methods of data analysis for reasons already discussed, they are empirical observations nonetheless, and finding ways to process them constitutes one of the critical challenges currently confronting psychoanalysis as a scientific discipline.

Working with the psychoanalytic process and taking the nature of that process into account, I have been attempting to develop ways of dealing with the observational data that will make appropriate use of their rich complexity and at the same time permit extraction of functional mind principles that can be meaningfully related to functional brain principles as they are known to us from the findings of modern neuroscience. (The intensive parallel study of relevant literature in cognitive neuroscience is reviewed in part

III.) The effort is still in progress, far from completion but far enough along to warrant a substantive progress report, which is exactly what this book represents.

CLINICAL EXAMPLES OF THE ROLE OF THE ANALYST'S MEMORY

The clinical examples have been organized to illustrate the developing approach in action. They report both content and process in analysand and analyst, using my memory of the analytic interactions as the source of the text to be studied. In discussing the examples, I have tried to indicate how attention to these memory phenomena in the analyst in some instances led to deepened understanding and increased accuracy of interpretations and thus facilitated development of insight in the patient. This focus on the role of the interaction between the memory networks of patient and analyst is intended to illustrate how the concept of the nodal memory network can be extended to include this new dimension; it is not intended to imply a recommendation for undue emphasis on it in actual clinical work.

To convey the evolution of the approach and the ideas as they developed, a series of clinical accounts will be presented and discussed in the chronological order in which they occurred. In each of the examples there were connections to one important, highly condensed, affectively charged node in my memory network. The first three examples contain further retrospective reflections about the case study that generated the questions addressed in the present work. A detailed and more complete report of the work with this patient—Carol—is available in an earlier publication.* Only as

---

*The text of the case of Carol has been drawn in large part from my previous publication, Reiser, *Mind, Brain, Body: Toward a Convergence of Psychoanalysis and Neurobiology* (New York: Basic Books, 1984).

much background material will be included here as is necessary for discussing the new issues and dimensions to be addressed.

Example 1: A Recollection from the Patient's Past

The first clinical example is of an instance of remembering something from the patient's past experience and communications that "belonged with" problems currently in the foreground of the analysand's mind. Carol, a thirty-four-year-old white businesswoman, came to psychoanalysis because of an inability to fall in love and marry. She was attractive to and interested in men, but each time a man became "romantic," she would find herself irritable and "bitchy," then anxious and angry, as if she were being attacked. Finally she would provoke arguments and a breakup, only to start the cycle again with a new man.

Carol's mother had died suddenly and unexpectedly while giving birth to Carol's brother when Carol was four and a half years old. The very last time Carol saw her mother was on a stormy night when her mother departed for the hospital. The newborn brother was placed in an orphanage, where he stayed until he was three years old. Only then was he brought into the home to live with Carol and her father, grandmother, and two aunts.

One rainy Sunday afternoon when Carol was thirteen years old, she and her brother were in the kitchen making tapioca. She put a large pot of boiling water on the refrigerator to cool. Her brother opened the refrigerator door, the pot fell over, and he was seriously scalded. The neighborhood physician who was contacted sent Carol to the drugstore to get an emergency medication to be applied before the ambulance arrived. She "awoke" three hours later, sitting on a bench in the park with a total amnesia for the intervening time. She had had a major hysterical dissociative fugue. She could not even remember the name of the medication she was supposed to get; in fact, since then she had never been able to remember it, though she had tried many times—a major disturbance of memory.

At a time late in her analysis, when Carol was engaged to be married and preoccupied with her longstanding conflicts about marriage and the possibility of becoming pregnant, she reported a two-part dream. In the first part of the dream, she was planning a trip to Europe and wanted to go to a certain city in or near Germany but could not remember the name. The travel agent could not help and referred her to another agent. Becoming increasingly frustrated, she asked to have travel guide maps of Germany. She would look at all the cities listed there, and maybe then she would be able to recognize the name when she saw it.

Then the scene shifted, and she was in the kitchen of her fiancé's home, with the whole family sitting around the kitchen table. She was naked but felt no shame or embarrassment. Her brother-in-law-to-be said, "That's a wonderful tan you have." At this point, she felt intensely embarrassed and for the first time in the dream she felt both guilty and ashamed. She asked for a robe.

This dream brought to my mind a past incident from the patient's life. The first part of the dream, in which she was distressed because she couldn't remember a name, reminded me of the incident of major dissociation when she could not remember the name of the medication—a name that had remained in repression ever since. She had told me about that incident early in our work, about four and a half years previously. I do not know why I remembered it at this time. Perhaps an empathic affect in me enabled the connection to be made. In many of the examples that follow, I can trace an affectively connected memory in my own memory system that seem to have resonated with an experience involving a similar affect in the patient's memory and in this way alerted or sensitized me to remember that particular incident from the patient's past.

The second part of the dream contained the word *tan*. I realized then that *tan*nic acid was a commonly used treatment for burns at the time of the accident. Could the word *tan,* which induced shame and guilt in the dream, indicate that the burn incident was on her mind, too? I told her I thought that this current dream, about not being able to remember a name, might contain a clue to the lost name of the medication from the burn incident. She remembered it immediately: "It was tannic acid!"

We can formulate that the word *tan* in the dream referred to the feelings of shame, guilt, horror, and fear that belonged to the burn episode and that the word was in fact part of an auditory percept that had constituted an important part of that experience and had remained in her mind as a mnemic residue of it. At the time of the dream, when she was anticipating marriage and possible pregnancy, that episode was very much on her mind, but outside of awareness. The word *tan* was heard again in the dream as a representative of the memory, but being only a part of the charged whole word (*tan*nic), it was heard out of context and so could escape recognition. In this way the painful feelings could remain latent.

Directing the patient's attention to the word *tan* and connecting it with the forgotten name in the burn incident enabled her to remember the whole forgotten name and to recognize the word *tan* in its other (that is, past) context. This recognition activated the original feelings at a time in her adult life when she could both experience them and cognitively identify their psychogenic roots in the past. She could then consciously reappraise the feelings as inappropriate and unnecessary in her present situation. This simultaneous cognitive and affective processing is an important aspect of the process of "working through" in psychoanalysis. In this instance, the process seemed to have been initiated by my recollection and then by the interpretation, which put her back into the earlier episode. Whether or not this formulation is correct, the observations stand as reported; if incorrect, the observations await an alternate explanation.

Example 2: A Memory from the Analyst's Past

In this example, a memory from my own past life clarified a current dilemma in the patient's mind by leading her to recall a relevant similar experience in her history. In the past, Carol had realized that if she ever became seriously involved with a man, she would have to bring him home to meet her family. She had a vividly detailed fantasy about what would happen. The family would all be seated around the kitchen table. In the course of the conversation, her young man would make a "terrible" grammatical error, and her family would be horrified that Carol had chosen a person so obviously uneducated and probably from a lower class. While she was aware of the unlikelihood of such an event actually occurring, she was not able to shake an inner conviction that it would, and she consciously avoided and postponed such an encounter as long as possible.

About a year after her analysis had terminated, Carol called for a follow-up appointment. She had not married her earlier fiancé but now was engaged again and felt that this time she was going to marry. Somehow she wanted to tell me about it. Everything about this new relationship was good; why couldn't she overcome her reluctance to introduce him to her family? The old fantasy was back in full strength: he would make grammatical errors, her family would be horrified, and she would feel ashamed. She knew it was nonsense, but she couldn't shake the feeling.

As I listened, I found myself remembering an incident from my own childhood, at age seven or eight—Carol's age when her brother was brought from the orphanage to live at home with her and the rest of the family. My recollection was of an occasion when my mother and other adults in the family were fussing and cooing over a neighbor's baby that had just been brought home from the hospital. With irritated indignation I asked my mother why she thought so much of that baby when "it couldn't even talk!"

Not only the incident but the feelings came back as well, and

69

strongly; I knew how Carol had felt then. And I thought I knew, too, how she felt now, bringing a new young man home to become a member of the family. If he couldn't even talk right, they wouldn't want him (a combined wish and fear).

I asked Carol then if she might not have made fun of her three-year-old brother's childish grammatical errors and wondered whether the memory of such incidents might have a connection with the unexplained fantasy fear that she was telling me about. She did in fact remember many such occasions and her secret delight in them. She felt relieved, and she went on to take her fiancé home and to get married. Did my recollection and interpretive question have anything to do with it? I conclude that it probably did.

Motivated remembering and forgetting is indeed mysterious. I wrote about this patient over six years ago, but at that time I did not remember having remembered about the neighbor's baby during that follow-up visit. It is only now, in writing this book, that I remembered it. (In the earlier book I did include the formulation to explain the fantasy, without remembering my recollection and the part it played in generating that formulation.)

Example 3: Recall of an Earlier Dream of the Patient's

In the final example from Carol's therapy, remembering a previous dream of the patient's and the analytic work she had done with it led to clarification of a newly developed post-analytic symptom. Several years after termination of her analysis, Carol (now married) developed a subway phobia under very stressful circumstances, the impending death of her aged grandmother, who had raised her after her mother's death. She returned for a consultation and in the course of it described the exact circumstances under which the phobia had developed. In listening to her account of it, a memory of a dream intruded itself into my mind, a dream that

Carol had told me seven years previously during her analysis. That dream had been a nightmare in which she was trapped in a locked toilet stall and awakened in a state of panic. In working with the dream at that time, she had recovered a memory.

The memory was of a visit to her mother's grave, at the age of eight. She had gone down a stairway into an underground toilet room a few yards away from the grave. As she urinated she touched the concrete wall, which felt cold and damp. She had the thought that her mother was just on the other side of that wall, and then she had a fantasy that her mother might have been buried alive and trapped underground in her grave. She felt suffocated; she panicked and ran quickly up the stairs into the open air.

The subway phobia had developed in the wake of a panic attack that occurred the very moment the subway car Carol was riding to visit her dying grandmother descended below ground level as the tracks carried it from the elevated portion into the tunnel. As she described its onset, I recalled the dream and reminded her of its content and of our analytic work with it (which, as one might surmise, involved conflicted, guilt-ridden death wishes and fears). After copious tears, accompanied by retrospective as well as anticipatory grief work, the phobia disappeared, not to return.

We can formulate that the perceptual impressions Carol received as the train carried her underground were very likely reminiscent of very similar perceptual impressions she had experienced and encoded in memory when she descended the stairs during the incident of visiting her mother's grave. The memory of those horrible moments must already have been stirred up by the grandmother's impending death at the time of the subway journey and then forced to the very edge of consciousness by the sensations generated when the train descended below ground. In this instance we see the overwhelming feelings of panic break through, leading to formation not of a dream image but of a symptom, namely a phobia. But the underlying principle is the same—perceptual memories connected in the mind by the potential to evoke the same painful, unacceptable feelings. As she ran up the stairs into the open air at the very first subway station, Carol thought, "I'll never go down there again!" The fear of being buried alive like her mother (originally connected to the cemetery incident) was displaced to the subway panic attack and finally to the subway, which now stood for it. The memory of the cemetery incident, along with its associated fantasy and the panic it could produce, could now be avoided by avoiding the subway.

Reminding Carol of the dream and the memory served as an interpretation, calling her attention to cogent memories that were at the moment outside her awareness. It appears to have guided her thoughts back to relevant nodes or sectors in her memory networks, thereby enabling her to work consciously with the archaic, unresolved conflictual issues under circumstances that permitted her to reappraise her feelings and her reactions to them cognitively. These old conflicts, when active outside of conscious awareness, had been able to generate unnecessary clinical distress and symptoms. When they could be consciously appraised in the current life context, they could be judged inappropriate and amenable to rational nonsymptomatic solution.

It also is probable that the experience of having her analyst remember her dream after such a long time could have had a strong emotional impact on Carol and may have played a part in facilitating her favorable clinical response. This, I think, would be a complementary rather than an alternative explanation.

It could well be asked how I came to remember that particular dream—indeed, to experience it as forced into awareness—at that particular time, which turned out to be so fortuitous. It should be easy to understand my own distress at that time. My former (successfully analyzed) patient had just developed a new and serious symptom. In addition to the intrinsic discomfort associated with the phobia itself, the symptom prevented her from going to work; her office could not be conveniently reached by any other form of public transportation. It was, of course, disappointing and anxiety-provoking for such a thing to have developed after all our hard and good work. I felt under great pressure.

Carol made a friendly joke: "Maybe I should ask for my money back." My anxiety manifested itself as an intense wish to understand and to solve the problem, heightening my attentiveness and concentration in listening to her description of the exact circumstances under which the symptom had developed. Could my feelings have played a role in what happened next? I can hypothesize that they did. My inner feeling state as I listened must have activated memories of similar, symptomatically active anxiety experiences from my own past, including ones of separation from mother (to be described in the examples that follow), putting me in empathic resonance with her. These empathic feelings could also have connected to another memory encoded in my mind, namely my memory of the nightmare and cemetery episode in her mind, which I had acquired from her on hearing the original account. In this way, an associative conduit could have been established between the two memory networks, enabling me to find the right memory and call it to her attention, thereby reviving it—and the feelings associated with it—in her.

Here, then, is another example of two memory traces being linked by shared affective potential, but in this instance two versions of the same memory in the minds of two different people. I hasten to add that this should not be taken to suggest anything mysterious, at least nothing more mysterious than empathy.

Example 4: A Mood in the Analyst

During the analysis of a young man (Richard), a mood connected with an anniversary I had forgotten sensitized me to an important element in the patient's dream, leading to the recovery of important new historical facts. One morning as I left home to drive to my office, I felt a strong desire to hear a particular song,* one that always evokes strong feelings in me. The wish was compelling enough for me to turn the car around and go back into the house to get the tape cassette and play it on the way. It elicited the usual strong response.

The mood persisted as I started work with my first patient, Richard. He reported a dream. There was something about the way he talked about one of the images in it—namely, his house—that caught my interest. I pressed for his thoughts about why that particular image might have appeared in his dream at this particular time. I didn't realize it then, but it became clear in retrospect that his mood in describing and associating to that image somehow fit with my own. It was one of rather deep but quiet sadness.

Richard's associations to the dream image of the house suggested that he was beginning to think that the young woman with whom he had a satisfying relationship might be planning to move in with him—seemingly a welcome thought, and hardly appropriate to the mood. This disparity heightened my interest and led me to inquire for further thoughts. He then reported that in the dream he felt that someone was looking his house over, as if perhaps to intrude. The color of the house in the dream was the color of his younger sister's hair.

This mention reminded me of the fact that his mother had developed a serious illness immediately after giving birth to his sister (the intruder?) when he was two years old. His mother had to be sent to a hospital for treatment that lasted about six months, and after returning, she had to spend much of her time in bed for several months more. Richard had told me that he thought his mother had been depressed at that time, but he had not yet talked about *his* feelings during that period. I asked if he could talk about them now and wondered if his mood in talking about the dream might provide a clue.

---

*Cora L. Diaz de Chumaceiro has written extensively on the role of melody and song in memory, particularly in relation to diagnostic and psychotherapeutic technique (Diaz de Chumaceiro 1988, 1990a, 1990b)

Indeed it did! He remembered how sad and lonely he had felt and how he had longed for his mother's return. We learned also that when his infant sister had been brought home, she had been moved into his room, and into his crib as well. The family had considered him old enough to sleep in a youth bed by then.

It appeared that the prospect of his girlfriend's moving in had reawakened the conflicts and feelings originally connected with the birth of the patient's baby sister. In his child's mind, her arrival had caused him to lose his mother. The session was a satisfying piece of analytic work, a "good analytic hour."

When I returned home that evening, my wife told me that after I had left in the morning, she remembered that it was the anniversary of my mother's death. I had forgotten and had not lit the traditional memorial *yahrzeit* candle at sunset the previous night. I had never forgotten it before. Of course I *had* remembered it unconsciously, and it had been unwittingly expressed in the compelling need to hear the special mood-inducing music—and in my sensitivity to the thoughts on my patient's mind. Would I have been as sensitive to my patient's mood and as persistent in pursuing that dream image on a different day, in a more usual mood and under less emotionally meaningful circumstances? It is not a question of great moment with respect to that particular analysis; our discoveries would have come to light soon in any case. But with respect to dreams, memories, and feelings, the episode does have a great deal to say.

Example 5: An Image in the "Mind's Eye"

During the course of an analytic session with another patient (Eve), a vivid image came into the my "mind's eye," one that carried a strong emotional tone connected with a highly significant period in my life. It leds to an interpretation that ushered in a significant period of work in the analysis. During that period the image returned like a leitmotif, heralding the appearance of further important issues and leading the way to further significant analytic work.

Eve, a thirty-six-year-old botanist, entered analysis because she was unable to solve her longstanding, intense conflict about pregnancy and motherhood. She had been married for ten years to a zoological taxonomist. The marriage was good, her husband shared her wish for children, and he looked forward to participating equally in parenting responsibilities. Recently they had moved to a new community to assume positions in a major university. The new work situation provided academic and financial advancement for both. Eve realized that she could no longer find any rationalization for postponing childbearing. She felt pushed, too, almost desperate, because of her advancing age: "my biological clock is running." Sex was satisfactory; she just could not bring herself to discontinue practicing birth control, much less make deliberate planned efforts to conceive. She could not understand her conflict and was feeling increasingly depressed and anxious.

Early in the second week of analysis, Eve reported a vivid and disturbing dream.

The Vulture

There was a man looking out a high window. I wanted to get to him, but I was in the grasp of a large vulture and was being carried away. The claws hurt. The man's look implied "Just hold on—you can get back to me." I was high up in the air; the vulture was holding me safe from falling, but it was also keeping me away from him. I woke up horrified.

When I asked Eve for her associations to the dream, she was able to make several significant connections.

I was horrified at the vulture (they eat dead people) and embarrassed to tell you the dream. . . . Yesterday I was angry with S. [a collaborator]. She reminds me of Mother—clings and won't let me go. Mother didn't want me to move here. She wants me to live near her. She is ailing and feels she needs me nearby.

The man in the window had dark hair—could he be you? I read in the university newsletter about a psychoanalytic symposium on "insight." The man in the window had "outsight"—he was *looking out* the window.

When I was little, Mother would threaten to leave when she was angry with me. She would get in the car (a station wagon) and back out the driveway. I remember looking out the window and watching her drive off, but she always came back. The dream is just how I feel—suspended, wanting to be here working on my problem with you; at the same time feeling torn, wishing I could be with Mother. She makes me feel guilty; the claws hurt.

I thought her analysis of the dream was excellent. Indeed the dream did depict her current situation, especially her uncertainty about what psychoanalytic insight might promise or threaten. To the sophisticated reader, the dream may seem hardly disguised, its meaning and significance far from obscure. But as will become clear shortly, the dream alluded to deeper issues, issues that are not so immediately apparent. They are represented by two elements of the manifest dream: being suspended high up in the air and the frightening bird. These two images reappeared in the first of two dreams that occurred as a pair fourteen months later.

1. Escape
I was being held captive but not hurt by a woman. I was in the back of a station wagon and wanted to escape. It was up in the air like the bird dream. I did get out and went into a house to hide under a table, screened by the tablecloth hanging over the side. A nice woman came in but didn't find me. Then two dogs (my pets, babies) came in and found me. The woman then knew I was there, but it was okay.

2. Making Babies
I was taking care of an older woman who was sick, preparing food for her in the kitchen. A man was there. I was sexually attracted to him and had to pee. I sat down on a toilet and peed. The man peed too, and it got on me; I thought it was messy but okay. I woke up "turned on" and woke my husband to have sex.

Eve's associations linked the two dreams and provided links with the earlier dream as well.

> Did I think babies were made that way—men and women peeing together? I always thought birds had babies by peeing the egg out. Mother peed a lot when she was pregnant, and Father always catered to her, stopping the car to let her out. It used to make me mad—jealous?

Note that the language and ideas seem to belong to an earlier, childhood epoch of her life. The frightening bird image is referred to but not actually present in the manifest dream. She is still up in the air. (It came out at a later date that one of her first suitors, the one her mother liked best and had wanted her to marry, was an amateur pilot who often took her flying "high up in the air.") She is being held but escapes and isn't being hurt. Something has changed! Pet dogs enter as dream images, and baby birds appear in her thoughts. The woman captor is nice, and Eve is taking care of a sick old lady. What wasn't okay before seems okay now. She dreams about making babies and wakes up to do just that.

Let us go back and see what took place during the intervening period after the vulture dream. I will focus on the five months preceding this pair of dreams, particularly on the analytic work that led up to the dreams.

At the beginning of this interval, Eve was remembering how her whole world had seemed to collapse during her year in kindergarten, the year her mother was pregnant with her third child (B.). Eve, the eldest of three, was an unusually beautiful, vivacious, and charming child. As the first and only child, her life had seemed idyllic; she was adored by both her mother and her father, who spent many happy hours playing with her. They called her their "Princess."

Following the birth of her first sister when Eve was three, Eve's mother became depressed, and the previously happy family scene was further disturbed by the introduction of discord and quarreling between the parents. Her father became less available to spend time with Eve. He would defer to her mother to keep peace, leaving Eve exposed to her mother's irritable moods. After a few months, the mother's depression receded, and life returned to a state nearly as happy as before. Eve felt more secure, loved, and appreciated, still Father's favorite even though he was not as available as before. And she was not unduly resentful or jealous of her baby sister.

All of this changed with the third pregnancy, which was unplanned. Her mother was preoccupied, anticipating another postpartum depression and fearing that she would be unable to cope with three young children. Eve was unhappy and anxious at kindergarten, feeling secure only when Mother let her stay home and be close to her, but this would happen only very infrequently. By the time her second sister was born, toward the end of the school year, Eve's whole world seemed to have collapsed. Never again as a child was she to feel carefree; instead she was burdened with a feeling of responsibility for her mother's now-persistent unhappiness and with a sense of obligation to make things better.

This she tried to accomplish by doing her best to take the maternal role in relation to her mother and to her sisters, thereby hoping to ease her mother's burdens. Gone were the times when she could spend long hours with her father, in his basement workshop for example, sitting on a sawhorse watching him build and fix things.

To convey the nature of the analytic work during the interval under discussion, I have selected five interchanges as representative samples. It should be borne in mind that they are excerpts selected for two purposes: first, to follow and focus on one main theme, Eve's conflict about pregnancy, and to convey the gist of our discussions as we attempted to understand the roots of that conflict; and second, to illustrate the way in which interaction between the memory systems of the two participants appeared to facilitate that search, thereby providing a window for observing some otherwise unnoticed but important principles of memory function.

It should also be pointed out that although the excerpts are presented as dialogue to make them more readable, they are not verbatim accounts. I do not tape-record hours, nor do I take notes during sessions. These conversations are reconstructed from notes written immediately after the hours. They are, I think, quite close even in wording to what was said—enough so to demonstrate the phenomena I wish to discuss. (Such accounts are, of course, memory phenomena and as such could themselves be taken as data for separate study.)

The first excerpt contains a pivotal interchange that took place as Eve was talking about the startling change in her world when she made the transition through the kindergarten year to first grade. As I listened and began to empathize with Eve, a vivid image appeared in my mind's eye. It was of the famous fresco painted by Masaccio to depict the Expulsion of Adam and Eve from Paradise in the Brancacci Chapel of Chiesa Santa Maria del Carmine in Florence, Italy. Along with the vivid image of the painting, I experienced the strong feeling of dismay and abject despair that it evokes—just as I did the first time I saw it and every time since. I thought I knew now what it was that she had felt then.

But why did she seem to be dreading that she would feel that way again now?

MR: Sounds as if you felt like you'd been expelled from the Garden of Eden.

Eve: I lost my good mother, the baby came and it was never the same again. . . . Maybe I wanted a baby and that's what screws/ screwed [tenses merge] everything up. Maybe . . . I don't remember it.

MR: You don't remember it, but you enacted it. (Eve had "confessed" at the beginning of the hour that she had had sex the night before without taking precautions, although she knew that she had just ovulated. She was not yet committed to becoming pregnant and had not intended to take a chance; she just did it without thinking.)

Eve: Yes, just like I forgot my watch today—like when I was in kindergarten, time was not important then, must not be now.

It is not difficult to formulate an answer to the question "Why now?" She was fearing the return of that awful feeling—dreading the end of her paradise—because she was beginning to feel the full strength of her preemptive wish to have a baby and unwittingly to act on it. If that wish carried with it the expectation of feeling again the way she felt as a child, it could well account for the equally strong inner prohibition, the other side of her conflict—the side that was saying "NO! It is not okay."

I submit that it was not just a coincidence that the visual image of that particular fresco came unbidden into my mind at the particular moment that it did. The image of the painting had first been perceptually registered in my mind/brain almost thirty years earlier, very shortly after the death of my mother. My emotional response to it was particularly powerful. Interestingly, it occurs to me as I am writing this chapter that her death was not the first time I "lost" her. Just a moment ago I remembered an experience at age five when my mother did not arrive on time to call for me at the end of the first day of *kindergarten*! All the other children had been called for and were gone. I was afraid I'd lost her. The affect Eve was communicating activated a corresponding network of affect and nodal memory images of my own.

I hypothesize that the experience of remembering the Masaccio fresco and the feelings that accompanied it were part of the analytic process, my response to what she had been telling me, directly and indirectly, about her feelings at that time in her life. I hypothesize further that the affective memory network it activated in me played an important role subsequently in the further development of the analytic process. I do not mean to imply that the analysis could only have developed as it did because of this experience. It could have gotten to the same place by any number of different paths. It did not have to develop this way, but the fact is that it *did.* Having happened as it did, it affords an opportunity to make some interesting observations on the role of memory in psychoanalytic process.

To begin with, I can report that the experience of remembering the fresco most certainly influenced the way I listened to further data as it emerged. The image of the painting returned from time to time as a leitmotif announcing the advent of significant material: of guilt connected with an inner feeling of sin; of crime and punishment—"crime" commensurate in the mind of five-year-old Eve with expulsion from the Garden of Eden. (She had been raised in a devout Catholic family.)

A few weeks later, the feelings connected with her kindergarten were mentioned again.

> Eve: I feel very unwelcome at the lab; like nobody likes me or wants me. I don't know why. I'm doing good work, but it isn't recognized or appreciated. It's like when I started kindergarten. I don't know what I've done.
>
> MR: That's when B. was born, your mother was withdrawn, and you felt you'd lost your best friend. Maybe you thought it was your fault.
>
> Eve: Mother's best friend came to visit, and Mother let her hold the baby. I wanted to hold the baby, too, but she wouldn't let me.
>
> MR: You thought, "Mother doesn't want me to hold the baby." Did that mean "Mother doesn't want me to *have* a baby"?
>
> Eve: Is it time to go? Isn't the hour almost over?

The next excerpt occurred a few days later. The previous day Eve had ended the hour saying: "You are very good. Sometimes I'm very impressed with the things you say." Referring to that comment, presumably the way she said it or intended it to be heard, she began:

> Eve: I was seductive—sexually provocative—with you yesterday. I shouldn't be, I don't want to be. I need help—feel paralyzed by my conflicts. You could tell me what is best to do, but instead you are leaving [for summer vacation in a few days]. It feels just like when I was left in kindergarten. I just don't know . . . you could help, but you won't.
>
> MR: You have a theory why I won't?

82

Eve: Yes! Because I'm BAD. . . . I'm thinking of the end of the hour yesterday. Because I'm bad, I feel responsible for Mother's depressions and illnesses.

This theme continued the next day. The Masaccio image came back to me very vividly. It was time now to share it.

Eve: Yesterday, as I left, I thought you looked horrified, like you were thinking it's a good thing I didn't become a doctor—I might have killed someone, a mother and a newborn baby.

MR: When we first spoke of your feeling of having been thrown out of the Garden of Eden, the image of a painting came into my mind. (*I identified and described it.*) I find myself thinking of it again and believe we can learn from it. Adam and Eve were expelled because they had acquired sexual knowledge. I think it's time to add to what we already understand. It is not just the idea of having a baby—it is also the idea of sex, of making a baby that contributes to making you feel so bad.

Eve: Is it time to go? I'm glad August will give me a break from this.

Five months later, Eve was consciously committed to becoming pregnant, actively and deliberately trying to conceive but from time to time anxious whether it was the right thing to do. In the interim she had been working actively with issues of triangular jealousy and competition. Her anger was closer to the surface, and she was intermittently preoccupied with transference fears that I would disapprove, be angry with her, even that I might discontinue the analysis—desert her.

Eve: I'm remembering that first dream: You were standing on a high cliff and I was suspended in the air by a big bird with claws. It was Mother tearing me away from you, but protecting me—keeping me from falling. Why was the bird so terrifying and so big? I wasn't actually afraid of birds as a child. After all, most birds are much smaller than children. But thinking of them even now can be nightmarish; it fills me with horror and dread (*shud-*

83

dering) . . . images like the ones in the Hitchcock movie *The Birds*
. . . and like the wicked witch in *The Wizard of Oz.*

MR: That dream was scary, and so is talking about it now. I wonder
where you got that bird image to put into the dream; is there a
scary mem——?

Eve: (*Interrupting*) Oh! The bird!!! I can't believe it. I'd forgotten all
about it! (*excited and crying*) I was given a pet baby bird for
Christmas the year when Mother was pregnant with B. Friends
of the family had a wonderful pet bird. It had laid eggs. My
parents took me there to see the eggs, and I was allowed to pick
out the one I wanted. After it hatched, I got to take it home for
my own pet—take care of it, feed it, and everything. I fed it with
a small medicine dropper and carried it around with me all the
time. It was my first pet, my first "baby." I was so proud of it and
loved it so much. On Christmas morning I was playing with it on
the floor beside the tree. Mother came in and stepped on it,
crushed it—killed it!! (*Sobbing*) To make it worse, Mother became furious at me. She went into a rage, said it was all my fault,
that I shouldn't have let it out of the cage. I was furious with her.
I wanted to kill her!

It was that night, or the next—she couldn't remember which—
fourteen months after the vulture dream, that Eve had the pair of
dreams, Escape and Making Babies.

A REPRISE: THE CASE OF JIM

Before concluding this chapter, I want to return to another previously published case study, that of Jim (Reiser 1984). As in the case
of Carol, I will include only the historical aspects that support the
goals of this presentation: (1) to elaborate on one special aspect of
the dream as a vehicle of meaning, an aspect observable only in
analysis—that is, the dream as a means of communication from
patient to analyst; (2) to elaborate by furthter illustrations the concept of the nodal memory network; and (3) to emphasize aspects

not covered in the previous report, aspects that were not apparent to me at the time of the first writing but that add to the thesis under development here.* The account that follows has been condensed and reorganized to illustrate phenomena under consideration here, and some cogent details have been added.

Jim and his sister, two years older, were sent to an orphanage when Jim was five years old. His mother was dying of uterine cancer and had been transferred to the hospital for terminal care. His father, who had very limited financial resources, had tried to manage the home and children in the time available before and after work, but an unfortunate accident had convinced him that he couldn't manage. One afternoon after school, an ordinary sibling fight between Jim and his sister got out of control. Jim threw a soaking wet washcloth at her, and as she ran to dodge out of its way, she crashed through a glass door, severing a large blood vessel in her arm. Neighbors, hearing the commotion, rushed her to the hospital just in time to save her life.

When the crisis was over, the children were sent off to the institution to live. Jim, of course, was blamed, and subsequently carried the blame as well as a deep and enduring guilt within him. After two years in the orphanage, the children returned to live with the father in the home of an aunt, and later with the father and a series of stepmothers after the father's several remarriages.

Jim sought analysis at the age of twenty-eight because of intractable premature ejaculation, panic attacks with paradoxical spontaneous ejaculation (orgasm unaccompanied by sexual excitement, thoughts, or erection), and inability to hold a job for more than six to eight months. He was single and worked as a chemistry technician. He was a bright, attractive, and likable young man. His whole manner of relating conveyed friendliness and sincerity. Concerned

*A comparison of two different reports of the same case written up at widely separated points in time might provide opportunity for further study of memory and the psychoanalytic process: for example, of the influence of theory on observation in analysis and vice versa. I do not propose to pursue such a study here and now but offer it as text for anyone who may be interested.

about appearances, he was always clean, neat, and dressed in quiet, conservative style. He had many longstanding friendships, was close to his sister and her husband, and maintained close ties to his father. In all ways he considered it important to be seen as a successful person with conventional tastes and life-style.

For the first six months of his analysis, Jim did not present any dreams. Interestingly, he would lie on the couch with one foot on the floor, as if ready to spring up and run out at any moment. Then he reported his first dream:

> I was in a doctor's office, a Dr. Riker. My old friend Alfie walked in. I threw a pot at him and said "Get out of here! You are dead and not supposed to be here!"

Note that Jim had thrown a wet washcloth at his sister with dire results. Was that memorable motion saved in memory as a proprioceptive percept and reexperienced—albeit with a different missile—in the dream?

What about the pot? Where did he get that image to put in his dream? *Pot*, it turned out, was connected in his mind with Alfie, a neighbor two years older than he, whom he had idolized and wanted to emulate when they were boys growing up together. In adolescence, however, Alfie had gone wild: he first became involved with marijuana ("pot") and alcohol, then got into stronger drugs, hanging out with jazz musicians and shady late-night characters, and finally ended in addiction, sexual perversions, and trouble with the law. (The institution where juvenile offenders are sent in New York City is on Riker's Island.) Jim, being younger, had been left out. He was envious at first, then disapproving and glad to have been left behind, but preoccupied and fascinated by descriptions of the wild escapades.

Alfie began acting strangely and eventually was committed to a state hospital with a diagnosis of schizophrenia. There he committed suicide. Jim heard stories about autopsies with their blood and guts and smells and was horrified by the imagined image of his friend in that scene.

It seems clear that Jim wanted to get the memories of Alfie and his "craziness" out of his dream and out of Dr. Riker's (Reiser's) office—out of his analysis?—lest he too be sent away again. As a matter of fact, his feelings about the institution to which he had been sent as a child were mixed. He became quite attached to it in many ways; it was calmer and more predictable than his troubled home had been. Already the model good boy, he quickly became the matron's favorite. Eventually he began to worry about being sent away from there, too, because he wet the bed at night. He would go to great lengths to change the bedclothes in the middle of the night to avoid being caught. One thing that bothered him most, about both premature and paradoxical spontaneous ejaculation, was the sensation of wetness and having it be noticed that his pants were wet.

Let us follow this associative path centripetally to memories and events from earlier epochs. Eventually it should lead to crucial early traumatic life situations and experiences that occupied a nuclear position in the nodal memory network that underlay many of his symptoms and character traits. This process will entail drawing on information available from all phases of his analysis.

Every time Jim attempted intercourse, he would have a premature ejaculation. Over the years he had tried to overcome it, compulsively and repeatedly, with great anxiety. Often the thought "What's wrong with me?" would torment and haunt him; he came to think of the symptom as a perversion and to be deeply ashamed of it. Often, in anxious foreplay, he would hurriedly open his pants and press against his partner's buttocks or breasts, pretending that the orgasm that resulted was what he had desired, so that he would feel less embarrassed.

Several months after the pot dream (he was dreaming regularly now and had both feet on the couch), Jim brought in the following dream:

87

> I was in a primitive wild African jungle, being chased by a headhunter. I was running after a buxom native woman and anxious to get away from the headhunter; I caught up with the woman excited and breathless. I began to come, and as I did so, I shoved against her backside like I often do.

He thought the woman represented a nurse with whom he had been having repeated experiences like the one in the dream. She had taken care of him during a recent brief hospitalization, when he had undergone diagnostic cystoscopy because of blood in his urine. (It was found to be due to a benign prostatic condition of unknown cause and required no further treatment.) Jim had not wanted to tell me (his "headshrinker/'haunter'") about her; he had felt particularly embarrassed to have taken up with a nurse he had met when he was her patient.

Another dream followed shortly:

> I was banging someone over the head with a sheet of metal, but it was thin and flimsy—like aluminum foil. I felt weak and impotent.

In associating to it, he recounted an episode of the night before. A neighbor in the apartment next door had recently begun yelling and screaming behind her locked door, disturbing everyone in the building. It was becoming clear to everyone that she was crazy and should be sent away. Since Jim was the person in the building who seemed to know her best, he was elected to intervene. He banged on her door, a thick fire door covered with a thin sheet of stiff metal. (Note the suggestion of the flimsy sheet of aluminum foil in the dream, and note as well the motor act of banging and the reexperience of the proprioceptive sensation associated with it in the dream.) She would not respond to banging on the door, so he had to call the police, who broke in and took her to a psychiatric hospital to be committed and sent away to an institution.

With great distress, Jim then confessed that for the first six

88

months of the analysis he had been secretly participating in daily (and sometimes more frequent) trysts with this psychotic woman in her apartment and not reporting it in the analysis. The pattern of their interaction, as he described it, was always the same. In the nude, she would serve him food, and while he ate she would hold, caress, fondle, and masturbate him to orgasm. She and her apartment smelled of feces and decay; she kept a pet dog that soiled the floor, and she would clean up after it only infrequently. It was after this had been going on for some time, without his telling me about it, that Jim had the pot dream: "Alfie, get out of here! You are dead and not supposed to be here!" In addition to reflecting his wish to ward off the thoughts, the dream could well have been an indirect attempt to tell me about the trysts.

The cystoscopy (a literally invasive, painful, and bloody attack on his already bleeding genitals*) occurred shortly after Jim had the pot dream. He terminated his meetings with the neighbor after the surgical procedure but immediately took up with the nurse. The displacement of the shame and guilt to the new affair with the nurse did not work for long, however. The headhunter dream seems, like the pot dream, to have been an indirect communication: Jim had felt that the eviction episode had exposed him in front of his neighbors, and he feared exposing his activities with the nurse to his analyst (the headhunter was chasing him). Finally, when he was unable to suppress the thoughts of shame and guilt any longer (by hitting someone—her? the situation?—on the head with a sheet of aluminum foil), these thoughts forced their way into his mind during an analytic hour via associations to the dream, and he confessed the facts directly.

Much later, toward the end of Jim's analysis, all this behavior was clarified. He had established a very satisfactory relationship

---

*It may be of interest to mention in this connection that his mother's condition—uterine cancer—is frequently accompanied by bleeding from the genitals, and the blood images had contributed strongly to his horror at the thought of the autopsy on Alfie.

with a young woman and was contemplating marriage. His premature ejaculation had for some time been resolved, but an annoying and persistent "small problem" had appeared. He thought that his fiancée had developed a bad body odor, but all sorts of soaps and deodorants had failed to remedy it. Soon it became clear that no one else had noticed it, and he became convinced that there was something "brewing" in him.

He brought it up in the analysis and mentioned having recently read, in a novel dealing with the exodus of the Jews from Egypt, descriptions of how some ancient Egyptian priests would perform sexual acts on the bodies of dead young women they were embalming. At first shocked and disbelieving, he was dismayed to learn, in looking into historical literature, that such things had actually occurred. He was at this time intensely interested in religious literature and art, particularly in accounts of the escape of the Israelites from bondage in Egypt and the idea of being forgiven as it was depicted in Renaissance art, for example, in moving portraits of Mary Magdalene, whose sins were forgiven by Christ.

It was in this connection that we came upon the highly significant new information. On Sundays during his mother's illness, Jim would visit his mother in the hospital with his father. The room was filled with the strong smell of the bandages soaked with blood and necrotic, purulent material. As the visiting hours drew to an end, his mother, reluctant to be separated, would hold onto him tightly. He would feel suffocated and want to be released and to escape (the exodus). He remembered now that these experiences were ones in which he felt a mixture of confusion and excitement, progressing, as they became prolonged, to excited panic.

One can wonder if his mother gave him treats to eat while he sat next to her. Were there also genital sensations? Did he wet his pants? Do these questions relate to his preoccupation with absolution from sin? We don't know, but it is not difficult to understand how the memory of these experiences, engraved in his child's mind by many repetitions, could have been revived in later adult situations of passionate sexual embrace and excitement and could have interfered with his sexual function. And the otherwise not understandable behavior of this conventional and fastidious man with his psychotic neighbor becomes understandable (even if unpleasant to contemplate).

The principle of nodal network organization of memory traces can be seen quite clearly here. The mother's sickroom can be regarded as occupying a central position toward which many of the significant symptoms, the symptomatic behavior, and the associative paths emanating from each of the three dreams eventually flow, linked to the center by shared affective potential including elements of love and passive longings for it, lust, guilt, shame, revulsion, rage, and finally anxiety—about separation, illness, and injury (castration).

Associative path in the pot dream:
pot → Alfie and drugs → perversion → wetness, enuresis, and smell → the psychotic neighbor → the mother's sickroom

Associative path in the headhunter dream:
head-haunter → nurse → the psychotic neighbor → mother's sickroom

Associative path in the aluminum foil dream:
aluminum foil → the psychotic neighbor → the mother's sickroom

THE NODAL MEMORY NETWORK: A SUMMARY

The clinical observations described in this chapter give rise to a formulation of putative functional principles underlying the storage and arrangement of memories in the mind:

1. Memories are stored and arranged in the mind according to (encoded by) sensory percepts registered during the remembered experiences.
2. Sensory percepts registered during states of emotional arousal are

stored in nodal memory networks organized according to the principle that percepts with the capacity to evoke the same affects (percepts with shared affective potential) are associatively linked.

3. The affective potential of a percept derives from the affect generated by the experience in which the percept was initially registered.

4. A single percept with affective potential is associatively linked with other percepts (belonging to different experiences) that have the same affective potential. Such a percept constitutes a node in the network, in the sense that percepts belonging to several experiences may be associatively linked to it (what Freud called condensation).

5. As life experiences accumulate, the nodal network expands, branches out, and becomes more complex. Percepts belonging to very early traumatic experiences constitute highly condensed nodes; later experiences are encoded by less dense perceptual nodes at greater distance from the earlier registered central percepts.

Note that all the functional mental principles listed above concern percepts. The idea of residua of sensory percepts appearing as images in dreams—taken together with the meaningful content of the free associations those images evoke—suggests how memories may be arranged in the mind: *Sensory residues in the mind are organized by affect and arranged as nodal memory networks.* This is the psychoanalytic postulate that emerges from the clinical data that have been reviewed. It is time now to see how the brain registers information and processes it for storage and retrieval, or memory.

PART III

BRAIN, COGNITIVE NEUROSCIENCE:
The Second Key

CHAPTER 6

The Brain Awake: Perceiving and Remembering

There Is More to Seeing than Meets the Eye

It would not be surprising if, to some extent, every perception were considered to be an act of creation and every memory an act of imagination. —(Edelman 1987, p. 329)

Having derived from psychoanalytic observations a hypothesis about how the mind works, we now turn to data from neuroscience. Part 3 will examine empirical studies in cognitive neuroscience and look for evidence relevant to that hypothesis. This chapter traces the path of visual images into the brain and shows how they are broken up for separate processing of various features almost from the start. It makes clear that these images must be reassembled for viewing and storage and that doing so requires high cortical and cortical-subcortical circuits, which are to be taken up in chapter 7. An interesting new perspective on imagery emerges, namely that the difference between waking and dreaming imagery is found to lie in this reassembly process. That is, the difference depends upon brain state, not upon the character of the perceptual residues per se.

From the study of dream phenomena, we know that the mind can do amazingly complicated things with information taken in from the environment. Patterns of sensory stimulation can be re-experienced during sleep in the form of hallucinated dream images. By contrast, a painting admired in a museum can later be vividly recalled in the mind's eye in the waking state, but no matter how determined the effort, it cannot be reexperienced as a real picture "out there," as it would in a dream or waking hallucination.

Clearly, perceptual patterns that stimulate the retina can be retained and reproduced, but when reactivated, the subjective experiences they evoke may differ in different states of mind—presumably different functional states of brain. Having recognized that, we must now ask how the brain could mediate such complex phenomena. The question becomes even more perplexing when attention is focused on mental phenomena such as the ones giving rise to the psychoanalytic postulate that a collage of dream images may be assembled and deployed for the purpose of symbolically expressing—and at the same time concealing—conflictual mental content. Here, indeed, is a quintessential mind/brain puzzle: how to relate mental (as we can know them from psychoanalytic data) to underlying brain functions (as we can know them from neurobiologic data). More specific to the task at hand, the problem we are addressing begins with questions about the individual imagery units that make up the dream collage. The clinical studies suggest that they are remembered perceptual units, residual parts of larger scenarios from past experiences. Where and how do these images originate? How do they get into the brain? And how are large scenarios and images broken into image units?

It is known that individual images may be fragmented into parts and the parts then used separately in creating a dream image. For example, Freud dreamed of a man with an elongated face "as though it had been drawn out lengthwise. A yellow beard that surrounded it stood out especially clearly." His associations led to the conclusion that "the face I saw in the dream was at once my friend R.'s and my uncle's." His uncle had an elongated face like the one in the dream; his friend R. had a yellow beard like the one in the dream. "It was like one of Galton's composite photographs" (Freud 1900, p. 139). How are the units routed, processed, and stored? How are they retrieved, reassembled, and reperceived in dreaming sleep? Are these latter processes during dreaming the same as, similar to, or different from image processing in the waking state?

Obviously, even elementary questions such as these cited above cannot be satisfactorily answered in full at the present time, but a great deal is already known about the biology and psychology of cognitive processes that is highly cogent to the issues in question. I am referring particularly to experimental studies that combine neurobiologic with cognitive psychologic techniques (cognitive neuroscience). Such studies will be reviewed in this and the following chapters. They are beginning to generate exactly the kind of bridging information that will be useful for checking psychoanalytic data and postulates about dream imagery against neurobiologic data about perception, memory, dreaming sleep, and dream imagery. The results of some of these studies, and the concepts they are generating, are worth examining in some detail.

HOW DO IMAGES GET INTO THE BRAIN?

Information from outside the nervous system (that is, from both the external environment and the internal environment of the body) gains entry into the brain when nerve endings in sensory organs are excited by the physical or chemical energy of stimuli such as light, sound, taste, touch, smell, proprioception, and temperature. Sensory organs are body structures—some very simple, others, like the eyes and ears, complex—that transduce (convert) stimulus energy into the form in which it can be conducted by nerve fibers, that is, into electrophysiologic energy. Pulses of electrophysiologic energy initiated by and corresponding to the stimulus are then conducted and distributed along nerve pathways to arrive finally at modality-appropriate sensory areas of the cerebral cortex.

In the case of the special senses like vision and hearing, the first sensory areas reached are called primary receiving areas. Each primary receiving area contains neural nets made up of many thousands of interconnected neurons and an even larger number of synapses, the connections through which signals are conducted, via chemical neurotransmitters, between and among the constituent cells of the network. It is in the elaborate circuitry of the visual primary receiving area (area 17) that the patterns originally evoked by light stimuli and transduced by retinal cells into patterned neural impulses are first registered in the cerebral cortex. So far, so good: the information, albeit in an altered mode, is in. But it has farther to go. Only after the impulses have reached more remote sensory and association areas at the highest levels of the cerebral cortex will it be possible for the image of the stimulus to be "seen"— that is, experienced and recognized. Yet as we will see shortly, even more may be required. Reaching the highest levels of cortex may not, by itself, be enough.

HOW ARE THE IMAGE-CARRYING IMPULSES PROCESSED AND ROUTED?

When an object or scene is viewed, a veridical image falls upon the retina. Eventually (though it seems to happen instantly), an image is experienced in consciousness (that is, seen) and subjected to cognitive processing (for example, recognized). But is it a precisely exact replica of the image that fell on the retina? Surprisingly, the answer is probably not. Immediately after striking the retina, where the light energy is transduced to the electrophysiological mode, nerve impulses carrying information about various aspects of the image are processed separately by different cell and fiber systems. Separation of processing of different image aspects begins almost immediately in the lateral geniculate body, which lies close behind the retina, and seems to increase progressively as the highest cortical sensory areas are approached.

Margaret Livingston and David Hubel have conducted studies in which

> Anatomical and physiological observations in monkeys indicate that the primate visual system consists of several separate and independent subdivisions that analyze different aspects of the same retinal image: cells in cortical visual areas 1 and 2 and higher visual areas are segregated into three interdigitating subdivisions that differ in the selectivity for color, stereopsis, movement, and orientation. The pathways selective for form and color seem to be derived mainly from the parvocellular geniculate subdivisions, the depth- and movement-selective components from the magnocellular. At lower levels, in the retina and in the geniculate, cells in these two subdivisions differ in their color selectivity, contrast sensitivity, temporal properties, and spatial resolution. These major differences in the properties of cells at lower levels in each of the subdivisions led to the prediction that different visual functions, such as color, depth, movement, and form perception, should exhibit corresponding differences. Human perceptual experiments are remarkably consistent with these predictions. . . . Even though intuition suggests that our vision can plausibly be subdivided into several components—color, depth, movement, form, and texture perception—our perception of any scene usually seems well unified. Despite this apparent wholeness, studies of anatomy, physiology, and human perception are converging toward the conclusion that our visual system is subdivided into several separate parts whose functions are quite distinct.   (Livingstone and Hubel 1988, p. 740)

Stephen M. Kosslyn writes:

> Perhaps the most fundamental insight of contemporary cognitive science is the discovery that mental faculties can be decomposed into multicomponent information-processing systems. . . . Although ob-

99

jects in visual mental images may seem to appear all of a piece, when the time to form images is measured this introspection is revealed to be incorrect; objects in images are constructed a part at a time. Studies with split-brain patients and normal subjects reveal that two classes of processes are used to form images—ones that activate stored memories of the appearances of parts and ones that arrange parts into the proper configuration.   (Kosslyn 1988, p. 1621)

It is true that images seem to be seen as whole and intact. If the apple in the corner is shiny and red, it will be seen as a shiny red apple in the corner. But we know now that various aspects of information such as those concerning the apple's texture, color, configuration, and location will have been dispersed to different areas of sensory cortex for analysis and processing and that the image seen will have been assembled one part at a time. And, as we will see in discussing memory, the information does not seem to be stored in a form or location where, like a photographic negative, it could be developed into a picture for viewing. Rather it appears that neural information from the retina is broken into components and routed through different neuronal subsystems and cortical areas.

So we come to the next question: How are these components reassembled to evoke a satisfactorily intact image? Apparently the brain is capable of doing what all the king's horses and all the king's men could not accomplish. Let us see how it puts Humpty Dumpty back together again.

GETTING IT TOGETHER

For the separate aspects of the image to be brought together and experienced as whole requires additional processing and involvement of brain areas and structures other than those so far discussed. This is where the story becomes much more complicated.

It turns out that the additional brain areas and systems involved in the perceptual task of getting the image together are the very same areas, structures, and systems involved in memory and emotion. Perception, memory, and emotion seem inextricably entwined. And to make matters worse, it is not yet known exactly how and where overlapping aspects of these three functions are carried out and coordinated. Nor is it clear whether or how separate structures and mechanisms are involved or whether separate structures are shared, and if so, when and to what extent? At the very least, some aspects must be carried out separately. The point was made in the General Introduction that the same tissue cannot be responsible for both perceiving and remembering at the same time. Yet as we will see in the next chapter, some of the same brain areas and structures *are* intimately involved in both! Are there different mechanisms? Do they occur at different times? Although the situation is complex and confusing, there are facts that will help. But before reviewing them, it may be helpful to clarify more exactly the nature of the problem at hand by offering an analogy to more familiar phenomena.

Think of the dream as a scene viewed on a television screen, with the viewing surface of the picture tube serving as the analog of the mind/brain's "perceptual screen." Images are immediately replaced by others in a succession fast enough to be seen as a moving image if spatial configuration changes (or stationary if it stays the same). The picture is accompanied by synchronized sound, broadcast on the same multiplexed carrier signal. The screen conveys multiple visual qualities of the image—color, shape, texture, position, and so on—and the speakers reproduce the audible sound qualities. Information about the various aspects of sound and visual images is carried in the broadcast signal and processed in audio and video circuitry, which then passes it along to the screen for viewing and to the speakers for listening. The technology of transmission and reception is capable of producing an integrated performance without outside help, but so far without memory. For that you have to add a separate system—for example, a videocassette recorder (VCR), which can record, save, and then retrieve the information when you push the "play" button. Perception and memory are thus served by entirely separate instrumental systems.

Not so in mind/brain; the same anatomically discrete circuits and tissues seem to serve both functions, possibly by time-sharing the same circuitry or by using different mechanisms among multiple mechanisms residing in the same tissues. In any event, if anatomically discrete tissue is shared, there must be some way for functional separation to be achieved so that each image can be perceived *and* passed along to memory at the same time that the perceptual screen is cleared for the next image.

Thus the analogy to television viewing breaks down quickly. It was deliberately chosen because it does so. The contrast between the familiar household miracle of television and the unfamiliar biological miracles under discussion here should dramatize the complexity of the phenomena that we are trying to understand. Yet the more that we can know about them, the closer we will be to understanding them and hence the closer to formulating plausible psychobiological models of dream formation.

There will be additional aspects of perception and memory to contemplate as further data come up for review. For example, the organization of stored sensory information in the various modalities is strongly influenced by the experiential context in which the sensory images were registered (Tulving 1983, 1989). Images in all modalities registered during an experience—for example, several parts of a landscape, accompanying sounds, smells, words, sensations of movement, and so on—tend to be recalled together. Recalling one facilitates remembering others. This effect may be enhanced by the strength of the feelings associated with the experience, and its influence may even be observed in the organization of dream images. But this is getting ahead of the story; it's time to pause and check our bearings.

LOOKING BACK AND LOOKING AHEAD

The first three questions posed earlier in this chapter have been answered in a preliminary way in our review of data concerning the origin of mental images in sensory stimuli and the entry of information about those stimuli into the brain. It is clear that perceiving and remembering regularly involve brain mechanisms that separate images into parts for analytic processing and mechanisms that reassemble the parts for viewing. This means that the presence of fragments or parts of images in dreams requires no special explanation. They are there as part of normal perceptual function; one does not have to be asleep for them to be there, available for use in constructing the dream. What is different about dreaming and does warrant special investigation is the reassembly process, which can—and so often does—produce strange and bizarre images. Extraordinary images in dreams are composed of things, and parts of things, originally perceived and experienced in ordinary ways. How is this to be understood?

Having gotten this far, and thereby having gained an appreciation of how intimately memory and perception are intertwined, we are now ready to address the second set of questions posed earlier in the chapter. How are imagery units routed, processed, stored, retrieved, reassembled, and reperceived in waking states and in dreaming sleep? In what ways are these processes similar in the two states? In what ways are they different?

Obviously, final answers will not emerge, but it is truly surprising and exciting to realize how much is already known and how rapidly cogent new data are developing. There are already more than enough to warrant pinpointing some observations and facts that should be taken into account in reevaluating older theories and in making comparative judgments between them and revised or new alternative theories.

The next chapter will present a selective review of material culled from the broader literature with a specific aim in mind: to focus specifically on phenomena that are relevant to the questions posed earlier. If those questions are the right ones, and if close examination of the phenomena help to clarify some obscurities, the endeavor should bring us closer to an enhanced understanding of the psychobiology of dreams and memory by assessing the relationship between state-of-the-art cognitive neurobiological and psychoanalytical ways of understanding the same phenomena.

CHAPTER 7

Perception, Memory, and Feeling

There Is More to Memories than Remembering

Most often memories originate as sensory impressions. Before one asks how the brain stores a sensory experience as a memory, one would like to know how the brain processes sensory information to begin with. —(Mishkin and Appenzeller 1987, p. 2)

The hero of this story is a monkey. We owe him a large debt of gratitude—and a share of the credit—for his mind/brain work in some highly important computations and discoveries. This monkey and others like him, in collaboration with Mortimer Mishkin and colleagues at the National Institute of Mental Health (NIMH), helped point a way toward learning things that we always wanted to know about mind/brain but didn't know enough to ask.

THE ONE-TRIAL OBJECT RECOGNITION TEST

Seated comfortably in Mishkin's laboratory, the monkey is taking a "one-trial object recognition test" (see figure 7.1). He sees a distinctive object (a circular block of wood), which has been placed over a food well in the center of the table within his reach. The food

FIGURE 7.1 One-trial object recognition test. Reprinted, by permission, from Mishkin and Appenzeller, *The anatomy of memory, Scientific American* 256 (6).

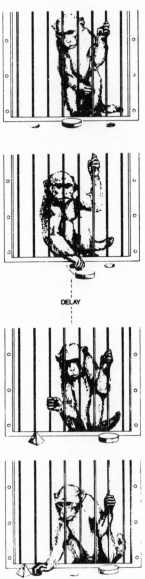

well under the block contains a peanut. Surveying the situation, he moves the block, picks up the peanut, and eats it. The block is then taken away.

After a ten-second delay the very same object is placed over one of a pair of food wells, located on either side of center. At the same time a second, equally distinctive object—a pyramid, the "novel object"—is placed over the second side well. Only one of the two side wells contains a peanut; to get the peanut, the *novel* object must be moved (the familiar, previously baited object is to be let alone). The curious monkey moves one of the objects and does or does not get the peanut (wins or loses); the objects are then removed (end of trial #1).

Twenty seconds later the same procedure is repeated; a "first object" is placed over the center well, the monkey gets a peanut, the object is removed, and ten seconds later this object and a second, "novel" object are placed over the side wells with the novel object over the peanut. This time, however, an entirely new and different pair of objects is used. Twenty seconds after the "decision" (end of trial #2), another trial, the same "delayed nonmatching-to-sample" procedure, is repeated until twenty trials have been completed, each with a new pair of objects.

Another series of twenty trials will be repeated the next day and on subsequent days, always with new pairs of objects on each trial, until the monkey learns the principle: namely, to move the novel object of the pair in order to get the peanut. The criterion for having learned it is making 90 percent correct choices. (As one watches from behind a one-way mirror, it often looks as if the monkey is enjoying the game, appearing to grin when he succeeds and relishing both the win and the peanut.)

Note that success on the task involves:

1. *perceiving* the distinctive features of the first object,
2. keeping its image in mind (*remembering* it) for ten seconds, after having seen it only once,

3. *recognizing* it the second time,
4. *perceiving* the distinctive features of the second (novel) object,
5. *comparing* the two objects and *distinguishing* between them,
6. *remembering* which was the original and which the novel object,
7. after being confronted repeatedly with the same type of problem, *thinking* it through ("computing" in Artificial Intelligence terms) to *recognition of the principle,* and last but not least,
8. wanting to do it (*motivation*)—satisfied curiosity and a peanut as reward.

Most monkeys, being inquisitive by nature, require only a few days to learn the principle.

USE OF THE TEST IN COGNITIVE NEUROSCIENCE RESEARCH

One might ask what this experiment has to do with dreams and why it has been described in such detail. The answer is that it has everything to do with dreams, and the detail is provided in order to underline and emphasize the fact that multiple and highly complex mental operations are involved in the test and that they must, at least to some extent, be sequential—that is, separated in time. If so, should it not be possible to study them, even tease them apart, through the use of cognitive experimental techniques? And should it not also be possible, through the use of neurobiological techniques, to carry out parallel investigations of the anatomy and physiology of brain systems and mechanisms that underlie and correspond to these mental operations? That is exactly what Mishkin and his colleagues have done.

Armed with detailed knowledge of the anatomy and physiology of the visual processing, memory, and affect systems of the monkey brain, as well as with the requisite surgical, physiological, electronic, and other instrumental and technological skills for studying and extending knowledge about these systems, Mishkin and his colleagues have applied their knowledge and skills in combination with cognitive psychological methods (cognitive neuroscience). Their general research strategy follows a pattern: Anatomical tracer studies and other anatomical techniques identify the neural circuits involved in specific mind/brain functions. Using techniques that monitor electrical and metabolic activity of the brain, they determine which cells and regions are most active during the performance of specified learning and other cognitive tasks, such as the discrimination and recognition of even such complex stimuli as faces and expressive facial features.

These studies pave the way for determining the actual functional importance of individual circuits and structures that have been identified. The latter kinds of determinations are carried out through the administration of learning tests to animals after the designated brain regions (or pathways connecting them) have been removed by surgery or modified by drugs with known pharmacological effects. This research strategy has made it possible to isolate various components of perception and memory (for example, registration, retention, recall, recognition, and discrimination), to determine which ones are impaired after each of the experimental procedures, and thereby to demonstrate the functional importance of specified brain regions and structures for specified aspects of perceptual and memory processing.

If we are ever to understand the psychobiology of dreams, we will have to understand how they are created in mind/brain from bits and pieces of information, information originally taken in by the senses and stored in a way that permits it to be retrieved and reexperienced afresh in the dream. To understand this will in turn, as Mishkin and Appenzeller (1987) point out, require knowledge of how the brain processes sensory information. The facts uncovered in Mishkin's research program are highly valuable, even spectacular in many respects, especially in supplying the kind of information that has for so long been sorely needed for approaching ques-

109

tions such as those posed in the preceding chapters. It is high time, then, to review them.

The review that follows will focus on findings and issues relevant to the central topics under consideration in this book. With the description of the "linchpin" learning task (the one-trial object recognition test) and the account of the overall research strategy, I have attempted to avoid the necessity of describing individual procedures and data analysis. Inferences and speculations will, however, be identified as such and set apart from the observed facts.

The program is an extensive and longstanding one. It has involved collaboration of many scientists representing multiple disciplines, both outside of and within the Laboratory of Neuropsychology at NIMH. A selective review, such as the one to follow, cannot possibly do justice to it. The detailed findings are covered in these articles and in Ungerleider and Desimone (1986), Friedman et al. (1986), and Friedman (1983). Readers with special interest in evaluating the work for themselves will want to consult Mishkin (1982) and Mishkin and Appenzeller (1987). I strongly recommend the second article to anyone with continuing general interest.

TRACING VISUAL INFORMATION

The processing of visual information can be divided into three stages.

Stage 1: Retina to Striate Cortex

Visual information is processed in the retina and passed back along the optic nerve to the *geniculate body,* a paired bilateral structure, part of the thalamus, that is located deep in the brain and figures very prominently in the unique physiology of the brain during dreaming sleep. Functionally, the geniculate body is the first processing station for the impulses after they leave the retina and before they reach the striate cortex, the primary visual receiving area, located posteriorly on the surface of the occipital lobe. As we saw in chapter 6, although separate aspects of image information are already being analyzed by separate subdivisions of cells en route to and in the primary receiving area, all the information has been traveling together up to that point and is still confined to one cortical area. That will change quite drastically on the next leg of the journey.

Stage 2: Striate Cortex to Area TE

After leaving the striate cortex, the path divides into two main branches, each of which goes to a different region of the cortex (see figure 7.2). A dorsal branch goes to the parietal lobe, where analysis of spatial location occurs, and a ventral branch goes forward to area TE, located near the tip of the inferior temporal cortex. The ventral system, the one most thoroughly studied, processes the information for analysis of size, shape, color, and texture. It is the one we will now trace. As will be seen shortly, area TE is an extremely important area and a promising place to look first for answers to questions about the intimate interrelationships between perception, memory, and affect. But before we get to that, there are two interesting things to note about the flow of neural information from the striate cortex to area TE.

First, neural impulses are routed through multiple separate stations, such as the areas labeled OB, OA, and TEO on figure 7.2, where different aspects of image characteristics (size, shape, texture, color) are separately analyzed, in parallel and in various sequences, before being channeled finally into TE. As visual information is sequentially processed, moving forward along the pathway, individual neurons have progressively wider "views." Individual neurons in the striate cortex, like individual cells in the retina, "see"

111

FIGURE 7.2 The flow of visual information from primary cortical area (OC) through secondary areas (OB, OA, and TEO) to the highest-order visual area (TE) and from there into the medially located amygdaloid complex (amyg.) and hippocampal formation (hippo.). For clarity, the hippocampal formation is pictured slightly dorsal to its actual location. Cytoarchitectonic designations are those of Bonin and Bailey (1947). Reprinted, by permission, from Mishkin (1982), *A memory system in the monkey*, Philosophical Transactions of The Royal Society of London B298:85–95 (p. 86)

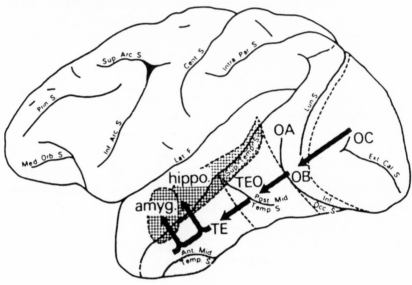

only tiny discrete features of objects and partial "views." By the time final stations of the inferior temporal lobe (area TE) are reached, however, individual neurons "see" whole objects and scenes, in which all the physical properties of objects (size, shape, color, and texture) that have been separately processed along the way have now been assembled and can be seen together. Remember, though, that information regarding location of the object in space has been processed along the entirely separate dorsal path from the striate cortex to the parietal lobe. For the complete scene, this information about where the object is will have to be brought together with information from the ventral path about what the object is.

Even in the awake state, the image is put together from parts, quite successfully but not so simply, it would seem:

> The observation that "what" and "where" are processed separately during perception leads to an explanation of why parts are imaged sequentially if the shape of each part is stored separately, and a part's location is specified relative to another part. If so, then one needs to have the reference part already activated before one can know where a subsequent part belongs in an image ... because one needs to attend to a specific place on the reference part in order to place a new part, and focal attention is restricted to only a single region of space at a time, only one part can be imaged at a time.
>
> (Kosslyn 1988, p. 1622)

In summary, information about the various physical aspects and location of an object is broken up and dispersed, with pieces of information somehow being stored in a form available for sequential activation and reassembly as part of waking perception. The inferences to be drawn seem clear. The first is that the dream process itself, as noted earlier, need not have anything to do with making part images; they seem to be ready-made for it. This leads to the question of how to account for the difference in the reassembly result achieved by the sleeping mind/brain from the result achieved by the waking mind/brain. The question is: Even if dreaming sleep fills other more primary basic survival functions (as we will see in chapter 11), could evolution have left us with a state-dependent process (dreaming sleep) which, as a by-product with no discernible survival advantage, constructs bizarre, crazy-quilt scenarios? It is possible, of course, but is it likely?

The second interesting point about the flow of neural information in Stage 2 is that as imagery information is carried forward toward TE, traversing thousands of synapses, certain neurons along these pathways transmit information not only forward but also backward to immediately preceding staging areas. Signals carried by these feedback connections go to cells in different columnar layers from the layers they came from in the preceding areas (Friedman 1983; Friedman et. al. 1986; Ungerleider and Desimone 1986).* These feedforward-feedback connections are extensive, and their pattern is quite regular, suggesting a special function. That function is entirely unknown, but it is a tempting subject for some far-out speculation. Considering that passage of impulses across synapses modifies the functional state and conduction characteristics—in short, the strength—of those synapses (Kandel 1979), it is interesting to speculate that patterns of sensory processing, delineating parts of objects in various stages of "dress" and "undress," might be retained in circuits that ordinarily process perceptual images after they have left the striate cortex and are en route to area TE. Could such patterns of processing be reactivated in dreaming sleep and participate in the formation of dream imagery if and when the main direction of excitation flow in these pathways is in the opposite direction from what it is in waking states—that is, back to the striate cortex rather than away from it?

In such a situation, neural information patterned according to earlier perceptions might—rather like frames in a movie reel running backwards—register on the striate cortex when they get there and so appear in the dream. Later, we will encounter the question of exactly how the dream hallucinations are generated. Remember, dream images are seen as real by the dreamer, and the eyes move as though watching something "out there," but the stimuli are not coming from outside, via the retina, but rather from inside, via paths that are not completely known. This issue will come up again after we review the neurophysiology of dreaming sleep.

It is finally time to get to the heart of the matter, to a series of

*Cortical columns—each a thin column of neurons (one-tenth of an inch deep and one- to two-thousandths of an inch in diameter), vertically arranged in layers—constitute the basic processing modules of the entire neocortex.

114

intriguing, provocative, and baffling problems: How does the mind/brain "get it together"—that is, organize the information for perception, storage, and retrieval (remembering)? What influences the choices of what to remember and what to forget? And what, if anything, do dreams have to do with such matters?

Stage 3. Area TE and Beyond: The Role of Neurobiologic Affect Systems in Perception and Memory

The amount of relevant information is staggering. The findings are fascinating and seductive to confront, providing some deep insights and promising even more to come, but all the same frustrating and insufficient to satisfy fully the curiosity of those who want to know all there is to know. Even a selective review will have to scan a broad vista of brain anatomy, stopping briefly to focus on quite a few structures, such as area TE, the entorrhinal cortex, the hippocampus, the amygdala, portions of diencephalon (the thalamus and the hypothalamus), the prefrontal cortex, other diencephalic structures, the basal forebrain, and the sensory areas of the cortex. There will be some new physiologic phenomena and concepts to encounter, just as was the case on the psychologic side.

Fortunately and appropriately, the topic of memory provides a unifying centripetal theme, just as the anatomical area we are approaching—a cluster of structures lying deep in the center of the brain—provides a functional center that serves to pull the functions of outlying anatomical regions together in the service of remembering. For purposes of discussing memory, this central anatomical cluster, which includes the entorrhinal cortex, the hippocampus, and the amygdala, can be referred to roughly as a unit, the *medial temporal lobe* (Squire 1987). Its extensive connections with the four "outliers" (prefrontal cortex, other diencephalic structures, basal forebrain, and sensory cortex) provide for functional integration of their memory functions. Note that the brain structures responsible for generation and regulation of emotions—the amygdala, the hippocampus, the diencephalon, and other parts of the "limbic lobe"—are integral, inextricable parts of this very same central memory system. Perhaps this last piece of information from the biological realm belongs with the postulate from the psychological realm that asserts that feelings play an important role in the organization of memories and in the organization of the perceptual residua that can represent them in the form of images.

INSIDE THE "MEDIAL TEMPORAL LOBE"

Severance of the connections of TE with more central subcortical parts of the medial temporal lobe results in serious impairment of performance on the one-trial object recognition test without compromising the capacity to make and to use visual registrations of objects, as in motor or *habit learning*. This latter form of learning (*habit memory*) utilizes direct connections between TE and motor systems that bypass the components of the medial temporal lobe. It is the kind of memory that is contained within learned skills; it is noncognitive, that is, it does not depend on knowledge or memories but on direct stimulus/response connections. It is like *procedural memory* in humans, the memory involved in driving a car or riding a bicycle.

By contrast, the one-trial object recognition test cannot be accomplished by habit or motor memory if the delays are more than a few seconds. The monkey must remember an object seen only once and know in a cognitive sense how to discriminate between it and a new one. It draws upon capacities for recollection like those used in what is called *declarative memory* in the human.

In other words, information that reaches area TE is sufficient for visual registration that can be used in noncognitive (that is, direct stimulus/response) ways but not for associating the perceived image of an object with a stored representation of it. For the latter to happen (and this is precisely what is required by the test), the connections from TE to amygdala, hippocampus, and medial thalamus must be activated, and further connections must be made from them to the prefrontal cortex. In turn, the prefrontal cortex must feed back to the very same areas of the temporal lobe cortex where the percept (now a memory) was originally processed and took shape. Mishkin and Appenzeller (1987) explain the process, which is also illustrated in figure 7.3:

> The subcortical memory circuits must therefore engage in a kind of feedback with the cortex. After a processed sensory stimulus activates the amygdala and hippocampus, the memory circuits must play back on the sensory area. That feedback presumably strengthens and so perhaps stores the neural representation of the sensory event that has just taken place. The neural representation itself probably takes the form of an assembly of many neurons, interconnected in a particular way. As a result of feedback from the memory circuits, synapses . . . in the neural assembly might undergo changes that would preserve the connectional pattern and transform the perception into a durable memory. . . . Recognition would take place later, when the neural assembly is reactivated by the same sensory event that formed it (p. 85).

Along similar lines, Harriet Friedman, Janice Janas, and Patricia Goldman-Rakic (1990) describe a network of brain regions that function cooperatively in memory processing in the monkey. This network includes both subcortical (specified thalamic nuclei and hippocampal formation) and cortical (prefrontal and cingulate cortex) components.

There are special aspects of both hippocampus and amygdala to mention here because they will be important later in the formulation of a conceptual psychobiological model of dreams and dreaming sleep.

FIGURE 7.3   Postulated interconnections and feedback in the memory system. Memory system was mapped largely by examining monkeys on a test measuring visual recognition memory (see Figure 7.1) after surgical damage to specific structures or pathways in the brain. The diagram at the top indicates structures that were found to be crucial . . . The chart at the bottom (based on a variety of evidence, including neuroanatomical studies of the circuitry linking the structures) shows how the structures might interact in the formation of a memory. A perception formed in the final station of a cortical sensory system activates two parallel circuits. One circuit is rooted in the amygdala and the other in the hippocampus; both encompass parts of the diencephalon and the prefrontal cortex. Each structure in turn sends signals to the basal forebrain. Through its many connections to the cortex, the basal forebrain could close the loop. It might precipitate changes in the neurons of the sensory area, which could cause the perception to be stored there as a memory. Reprinted (with modifications) from Mishkin and Appenzeller, *The anatomy of memory.* Copyright © 1987 by *Scientific American*, Inc. All rights reserved.

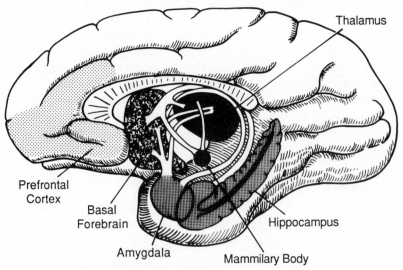

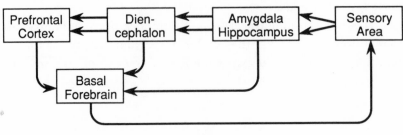

The Hippocampus

The known functions of the hippocampus seem related primarily to memory, but because of its immediate connections to other parts of the limbic system, its functions are virtually inseparable from those that generate and regulate emotions. Jonathan Winson (1985) refers to it as the "gateway" to the limbic system; it is where information from the neocortex is processed and then transmitted to the limbic system, where memory and emotion are integrated. This complex structure is known to play a central role in memory; indeed, in humans it is essential for retrieving memories for approximately a three-year period following registration of experience. During this period, the experience is being laid down and consolidated in long-term memory; after three years the hippocampus will no longer be essential for retrieving it.

The hippocampus must somehow alter the status of the stored information in some way during the three years. Patients in whom this structure has been destroyed by disease or by trauma suffer from a form of amnesia known as total or *global amnesia*. They cannot remember anything that happened to them during the three years preceding the onset of the disorder (*retrograde amnesia*), although they can remember things that happened before that. Moreover, they cannot lay down any new memories at all (anterograde amnesia). Anything that happens to them now cannot without rehearsal be remembered for more than a few seconds (Squire 1987; Milner 1962). The memory defect is circumscribed, in that patients can successfully perform very complicated cognitive mental tasks (the "Tower of Hanoi" puzzle, for example) but a few minutes later are unable even to recognize the puzzle or remember having done it. How the hippocampus accomplishes its memory-processing function is not entirely known or fully understood, but several phenomena are known to be involved in it that are appropriate to note here.

The first is *long-term potentiation* (LTP), a process observed to occur in certain hippocampal memory-processing circuits (and in neocortex as well). In this process, electrical stimulation of a neural pathway leading to a synapse results in a lasting increase in the strength of the postsynaptic responses of that synapse. LTP occurs under the influence of particular neural inputs to specific parts of hippocampal memory-processing structures and is considered almost certainly to be centrally involved in long-term memory. It has recently been demonstrated that LTP may be influenced by psychological factors and that it may be involved in behavioral learning processes (Shors et al. 1989). Details of how LTP works—via molecular mechanisms on the surface membrane and within the neuron itself—are currently under active investigation in several leading neuroscience laboratories throughout the world (Stevens 1989).

Next are two closely related phenomena that have important implications for understanding the functions of dreaming sleep: theta rhythm and neuronal gating in the hippocampus. These have been studied in detail by Jonathan Winson at Rockefeller University and reported in a highly interesting book, *Brain and Psyche: The Biology of the Unconscious* (1985), and in more recent articles (Winson 1986; Winson and Dahl 1986). Winson's studies of a variety of mammalian species found certain behavioral states and physiologic conditions in which a particular rhythm of brain electrical activity (*theta rhythm*) can be regularly observed in parts of the hippocampus. These sections are in an area where a key hippocampal circuit (the *trisynaptic circuit*) processes information arriving from the sensory cortex via the entorrhinal cortex, which collects from all areas of the sensory cortex.

From this collecting area, the signals are passed to the hippocampus for processing in the trisynaptic circuit and then to the limbic system, thalamus, and prefrontal cortex. When theta rhythm is present, the last cell group in the trisynaptic circuit does not pass it on, as if a gate were closed. The "hard wiring" of the circuit is the same, but its functional pattern (routing and passage of impulses within and through it) is different. This functional alteration in the circuit must be associated with fundamental changes in memory processing at such times, and it is important in dreaming because, as we will see, it always appears in dreaming sleep. A principal physiologic precondition for the appearance of theta rhythm in the hippocampus is transmission of neural impulses to it from lower brain stem centers. These lower brain stem centers exert their influence via aminergic neurotransmitters such as norepinephrine and probably serotonin. These same centers and neurotransmitters figure importantly in regulating vigilance and alertness in waking states, and they also are important in the neurophysiology of dreaming sleep.

It is interesting to note that theta rhythm appears only in specific waking behavioral states and that these turn out to be states important for survival in each mammalian species studied, different states in each species presumably because of their different behavioral patterns: exploration in the rat, exploration and predatory activity in the cat, exploration and escape-from-predator behavior in the rabbit. But theta rhythm also always appears in one other state in all three species, namely in REM sleep, the stage of sleep associated with dreaming in the human. Winson (1985) notes that

> The same neurons in the hippocampus are performing the same process characterized by theta rhythm during one other behavioral state, REM sleep, when there is no sensory input from the outside world; it is as if certain information gathered during the day, information associated with survival behaviors, was being dealt with again by structures in which theta rhythm is generated: the entorrhinal cortex and the hippocampus (pp. 190–91).

Winson has suggested that the hippocampus might, in dreaming sleep, engage in "off-line processing" of the day's perceptual input—sorting out important material for memory storage and discarding the rest, to be forgotten. This is an intriguing idea in

121

that it implies an intimate, biologically useful connection between memory and dreams. It will come up again in chapter 11 for extended discussion.

The Amygdala

The amygdala is an almond-shaped structure that provides the central crossroads junction where information from all senses is finally tied together and endowed with emotional meaning. This function can be understood to be possible because of the amygdala's extensive direct two-way connections: with all cortical sensory systems, with the part of the thalamus involved in memory, and with the hypothalamus, the key area deep in the brain where emotional responses are generated and governed. It is here that the sights, smells, tastes, sounds, and proprioceptive and touch sensations of an experience are brought together to be perceived and remembered. The amygdala's two-way connections with each of the cortical sensory areas allow information from each sensory area to be sent back not only to its own primary area but also to the primary cortical areas for the other modalities (see figure 7.4) These are the connections that provide for cross-modality associations: a remembered face may evoke the memory of the voice, smell, or touch of a person; hearing "our song" may evoke a flood of remembered sensations, experiences, and feelings, the stored memories of a treasured romance (recall Humphrey Bogart's demand, "Play it, Sam"). It is possible, too, that emotional associations mediated by these same connections could influence the shape of perceptions, by influencing the amount and kind of attention paid to different contextual aspects of an experience, and in turn influence which features are ultimately remembered or emphasized in remembering experiences, as in episodic memory (Tulving 1989).

Thus, it is in and through the cortico-limbic circuits of the

FIGURE 7.4 Multiple connections of the amygdala underlying the variety of roles it is thought to serve in memory. Fibers reach the amygdala from the final stations of cortical sensory systems. Sensory impressions thereby activate one circuit of the memory system, which depends on connections between the amygdala and the thalamus (a structure in the diencephalon) (not shown). Links between the amygdala and the hypothalamus (not shown), where emotional responses probably originate, seem to allow an experience to gain emotional associations. Those links may also allow emotions to influence learning, by activating reciprocal connections from the amygdala to sensory paths (shown here for the visual system only). The existence of connections running back to the sensory areas from the amygdala may explain why a single stimulus can elicit diverse memories, as the smell of a familiar food summons memories of its appearance, texture, and taste. Reprinted (with modifications) from Mishkin and Appenzeller, *The anatomy of memory.* Copyright © 1987 by *Scientific American*, Inc. All rights reserved. (p. 88)

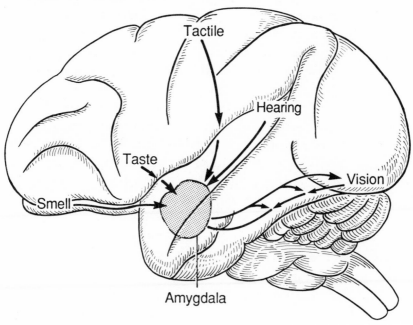

perception/memory/affect system that connections are made with the prefrontal cortex and through it with the entire association cortex. We may therefore infer that these are the connections through which experiences acquire meaning. This is to say that the emotional meaning of an experience could attach it to its current perceptual content and then to the past by bringing that current perceptual content into associational connection with previous emotionally meaningful experiences.

INFLUENCES FROM OUTSIDE THE MEDIAL TEMPORAL LOBE

There are two other important points to mention briefly before we close out this part of the story. One is the effect of neurotransmitters on the cortico-limbic systems we have been discussing. Norepinephrine originating in the locus coeruleus, which is located in the brain stem (pons), and terminating in the amygdala "tunes" these circuits up and down—sets the gain, as it were—making them more or less sensitive and responsive. In this way it influences appraisal of environmental stimuli—for example, judgments of whether a situation or object is threatening or benign (Aston-Jones and Bloom 1981; Aston-Jones, Foote, and Bloom 1984). Reciprocally, the locus coeruleus is the target of neural signals sent back from the amygdala, closing a feedback loop. Acetylcholine originating in the basal forebrain and terminating in all areas of the sensory cortex plays a vital role in memory. The basal forebrain also receives reciprocal innervations from the hippocampus, amygdala, diencephalon, and prefrontal cortex, closing still more feedback loops in the memory system. The memory system is replete with such loops, a fact that has implications for the nature of the processing operations of the system.

The second point to mention and emphasize is the vitally important role of the direct and immediate connections between the core of the memory apparatus and the hypothalamus, which is where the central control of autonomic and neuroendocrine stress systems is located. In addition to effects on emotional states and on physiologic systems throughout the body (Reiser 1984), activation of key hypothalamic centers can exert powerful effects on memory. Adrenal cortical stress hormones, for example, are known to enhance and strengthen memory processes (McEwen 1986, 1987; McEwan and Brinton 1987), probably by modulating neurotransmitter effects at the synapse. The survival value of such a biological mechanism will be obvious. The effect can be mild or strong, depending on the degree of alarm. In conditions of intense stress and excitement, the memory system can be subjected to a virtual barrage of neural, neurohumoral, and endocrine messages that say "Remember this!" Who doesn't remember exactly, and with vivid detail, where they were and what they were doing when they heard about the assassination of President John F. Kennedy or the sudden death of a family member or close friend?

It works on the good-news side as well. A personal story:

The One That Didn't Get Away

At this or any other moment I choose, I can recall every detail of *smell, sound* (bird calls, a loud splash), *sight* (the water's broken surface, a momentary flash of gleaming green, salmon-orange, and white, the tilted bow of the canoe, pines at the pond's edge); and *feel* (the abruptly taut line, my heart pounding in my chest)—all experienced at the exact moment when the 2¾-pound wild brook trout took the fly on August 14, 1984, 11:01 A.M. "Remember this!" I won't ever forget it.

AN INTERIM CONCLUSION

The experimental data from cognitive neuroscience (reviewed in chapters 6 and 7) and the data from clinical psychoanalytic process (reviewed in chapters 3 and 5) turn out to be quite compatible. Observations from each of the two realms, despite differences in the nature of the data, support a common functional principle, namely that emotion plays a major role in organizing storage of sensory information in both mind and brain. Surely this must carry important implications for understanding the nature of dream imagery. Let us move on.

CHAPTER 8

The Sleeping Brain

The Physiology of Dreaming Sleep

The 1950s is thus the decade of the establishment of a third major brain-mind state: REM sleep-dreaming. . . . The discovery that REM sleep is regularly recurrent, and that dreaming is its concomitant state of consciousness, opened the doors to a truly objective and instrumental investigative approach to the mind-brain question.
—(Hobson 1988, pp. 151, 154).

The dream would truly appear to be born in the brainstem but clothed in the cortex.
—(Roffwarg, Muzio, and Dement 1966, p. 13)

The late Gustav Eckstein, physiologist and biographer (of Noguchi and Pavlov), was famous for other accomplishments as well, among them his astute observations and insights into the nature of animal behavior (Eckstein 1936). He loved to tell the following cat story.

127

THE CAT WHO COULD TELL TIME

The protagonist, a sheltered family pet, always regular in his habits, developed a new behavior that startled his family, one that was quite out of keeping with his personality except for its regularity. He would disappear from home at dusk and return shortly before midnight. "Cherchez la femme," the family's first thought, seemed to be ruled out by the precise schedule he followed—every Monday and *only* on Monday, regardless of season and weather. After many months they called in Dr. Eckstein, who astutely followed the cat to find out what was going on.

The route led several miles to a high brick wall. The cat climbed to the top and sat patiently gazing into the windows of a church basement. After a short time the windows would light up, and soon a spirited bingo game would be in progress. When it was over, the cat would return home.

How did the cat know it was Monday? The answer is quite simple. He had a highly reliable internal clock, in fact not one but many: heart rate, respiration, and many other regular body rhythms that are internally registered in the brain. Under most circumstances they are not consciously perceived, but nonetheless they are registered and can be entered into time computations, as evidenced by the cat who could tell time.

So can we. For example, most of us have had the experience of waking up on time without an alarm clock when we have a train or plane to catch early in the morning.

BIORHYTHMS

The anecdote of the cat has been offered to locate the subject of the sleeping brain, and the special substage of sleep in which dreaming occurs, within the broader context of *chronobiology,* the science of biorhythms. The brief discussion of biorhythms that follows is intended only to sketch in a background for later discussion of the psychobiologic aspects and possible significance of dreaming sleep in that broader context, in chapter 11.

Physiologic systems within living organisms display multiple rhythms—regularly waxing and waning rates, frequencies, and amplitudes of individual functions—governed by intrinsic "pacemakers" and subject to influence by internal regulatory mechanisms and by internally generated and externally imposed stimuli and demands. Health reflects and ultimately depends upon satisfactory synchronization of the entire array of the body's functional rhythms. This synchronization is accomplished within the brain, which has its own intrinsically generated rhythms that are likewise subject to influence by internal bodily and externally imposed stimuli and demands.

The sleep-wake cycle reflects one of the major functional rhythms of the brain, and as noted in the first epigraph, the REM dreaming phase of sleep has been established as "a third major brain-mind state"—a window of opportunity for inquiry into mind/brain questions. With the use of modern electroencephalograph and polygraph instrumentation, it is possible to identify two alternating major stages of sleep: rapid eye movement (REM) and non-REM sleep. There are four depth levels of non-dreaming sleep (NREM) that are qualitatively similar. Typical visual dreaming occurs during the REM or dream periods. Thus the sleep phase of the circadian (twenty-four-hour) sleep-wake cycle contains a REM-NREM ultradian (less-than-twenty-four-hour) cycle. Kleitman (1963) regarded the latter as representing a basic rest-activity cycle. REM periods occur at approximately ninety-minute intervals. Usually there are four or five REM periods of roughly twenty minutes' duration during each night's sleep, usually shorter earlier and longer later in the sleep period. The ninety-minute ultradian rhythm seen during sleep may continue during waking hours, but with quite different psychologic and behavioral manifestations such as movement, eating, drinking, and smoking (Friedman and Fisher

1967). The period of this ninety-minute ultradian rhythm lies between the much shorter ones represented by cardiac rate (approximately one second) and respiration (approximately four seconds) and the much longer ones (twenty-four hours to thirty or ninety days) to be mentioned below. The longer periods of some of the body rhythms seem to correspond to cyclically imposed environmental stimuli; quite possibly such stimuli influenced the evolution of their intrinsic pacemakers. The twenty-four-hour circadian rhythm of sleep-wake, body temperature, and adrenal hormonal activity corresponds with rotation of the earth on its axis, producing night-day and dark-light cycles. The twenty-eight-day lunar rhythm of the menstrual cycle corresponds to the revolution of the moon around the earth. And the seasonal rhythms of ninety days, plus or minus, that are seen in animals in molting and hibernation and in humans in seasonal variations in mood and the incidence of certain diseases (for example, peptic duodenal ulcer and depression) correspond to the revolution of the earth around the sun.

A LOOK AT HOW FAR WE'VE COME

Consciousness and the four instrumentally defined stages of sleep and REM each reflect separate and different physiologic brain states. Being manifested both as a distinct state of consciousness and as a distinct state of brain function (with each aspect accessible to study by domain-appropriate methods), REM sleep provides a unique window for inquiry into some of the major mind/ brain questions central to the task of this book. In preparation for that inquiry, let us first summarize briefly the psychoanalytic clinical observations and inferred *functional mental principles* described in chapters 3, 4, and 5, and the experimental observations and inferred *functional neurophysiological principles* derived from the field of cognitive neuroscience, described in chapters 6 and 7. We will then review those aspects of the physiology of

REM sleep that seem relevant to the functional mental and neuro-physiological principles and begin to interpret the theoretical implications of the data.

This approach should provide a basis for comparing two separately derived sets of functional memory principles, one from the domain of mind and the other from the domain of brain, and assessing each set in relation to a single psychobiological state (REM sleep) and hence to each other. This assessment, in principle, will be required for the ultimate formulation of a satisfactory psychobiological model of dreams and dreaming. This particular phase of the study represents an effort to move in the direction of formulating such a model, but it is focused rather than general, concentrating mainly on one central aspect of dream process, namely the generation of dream imagery.

The Functional Mental Principles

Dream collages appear to be put together from parts of sensory percepts taken from different historical epochs of the dreamer's life. The perceptual residues are mainly visual, but they may also be in auditory, tactile, proprioceptive, and even occasionally olfactory and taste modalities. A person's dream images appear to be associatively connected with each other by virtue of shared emotional meanings and to be arranged accordingly in nodal memory networks. The remembering of percepts and the establishment of associative linkages between them seem to be based on the circumstance of having been registered during similarly disturbing life events when the feelings aroused by emotional meanings were strong.

Thus whole and partial percepts registered at different times and in connection with different experiences may in the dream reappear together as composite images and as parts of the same dream experience. When they appear, altered and rearranged, in dreams, these perceptual residues can be regarded as allusions to thoughts and emotionally painful feelings. Because they are perceptual allusions rather than linguistically rendered thoughts, it is believed that they can escape conscious recognition and thereby avoid activating painful feelings that could disturb the dreamer's sleep, as does happen in REM-stage anxiety dreams, when painful feelings are in fact activated (Fisher et al. 1970a, 1970b, 1973, 1983; Fisher, Gross, and Zuch 1965; Hartmann 1984).

The Functional Neurophysiological Principles

Information from the environment that is contained in sensory registrations (which have been studied in most detail in the visual mode) appears to be broken up for separate processing of its various aspects and then reassembled for perceiving and remembering. In the first phases of the process (stages 1 and 2), various image components are left behind as part image traces scattered in various states and stages of disassembly in prestriate occipital cortex and in temporal cortex. The term *part image traces* refers to relatively stable patterns of synaptic connections that are capable of being reactivated by virtue of having been traversed by the identical pattern of neural impulses once or many times before—the more times, the more stable the pattern. In the later phases (stage 3 and beyond), the images will be reassembled for viewing, storage in the association cortex, and retrieval.

The reassembly processes, which are influenced by brain stem centers that also control arousal and alertness, involve connecting fresh percepts with sensory percepts that have been previously stored in the association cortex. These connections are effected through the very same subcortical circuits and structures that are involved in processing emotion. It is in this way that the associative links are established. The reciprocally interconnected cortical and subcortical systems constitute complex neural nets containing multiple reentry paths, feedback, and loops within loops, arranged in overlapping progressions. The computations required in these cognitive functions are amazingly complex. A central question concerns the ways in which the retrieval and reassembly processes may differ, depending on whether the person is awake or is asleep and dreaming.

The anatomical and physiological arrangements in the brain have been compared to circuitry patterns employed in "parallel and distributed" computer processing systems (Mountcastle 1978; Rumelhart, McClelland et al., 1986). Such systems differ from linear artificial intelligence (AI) systems, which perform successive computations in series according to algorithmic (either/or branching type) logic programs. Despite the fantastic speed of modern computers, the number of serial computations required for cognitive functions such as those accomplished by the brain would require a greater number of computers than would be practically feasible and would still require far more time to complete them than does the brain.

In contrast, parallel and distributed systems distribute parts of the computations to a number of small computer circuits, which then carry out the assigned computations simultaneously (in parallel). The computations therefore take far less time, since they do not have to "wait in line." The separate, smaller computer circuits are interconnected in ways that enable the results of the parallel smaller computations to be combined for computation in higher-order circuits.

"Wiring" arrangements in the brain are strikingly similar. Individual neurons in a cortical macrocolumn connect not only with the other cells in that column but also with neurons in adjacent columns. And cortical macrocolumns are interconnected to constitute cortical modules that in turn connect with modules in subcortical circuits. Individual neurons are thus connected with many widely distributed modules and therefore with individual neurons in many circuits other than their own. Many modules share the same neuron, so to speak. (If we were to describe these neural nets as "nodal" and discern echoes of "condensation and displacement" in what has just been described, would we be doing semantic tricks, or would we be discerning isomorphic functional principles? I prefer to think the latter.)

There are further, even more puzzling issues. They relate to a fourth stage of perceptual processing: Where does visual perception actually occur? How do we become conscious of stimuli? How do we recognize and distinguish between different stimulus patterns, such as familiar faces? Vernon Mountcastle (1978) summarizes the complex processing computations involved up to and including the cortex.

> While intracortical processing within area 17 [the primary visual cortex, located in the posterior occipital lobe] is an essential step leading to visual perception, it is probably correct to say that visual perception does not "occur" there, but rather within a series of complex distributed systems in each of which a locus in area 17 is an integral part. For the most complex aspects of vision, a primate possessing only area 17 among all visual and visual associative cortical areas would probably be perceptually blind.
>
> Studies of the dynamic activity of visual cortical neurons suggest that within any given macrocolumn, processing for different stimulus attributes proceeds along parallel channels. The general rule seems to be that the attributes selected in a given pathway leading to an output channel are those further elaborated in the target area of the channel: the processing and distribution functions of a cortical column are then combined. (pp. 21–22)

All the circuitry and complex functions discussed above must be involved. But is there more? Are consciousness and thought emergent functions—emergent from these highest-level neural systems, dependent upon them but not fully explainable by them? I do not know, and I am not inclined even to guess or lean toward a preference. Instead, let us return to the real world and look at sleep.

RAPID EYE MOVEMENT (REM) SLEEP

In the typical sleep laboratory, an array of recording surface electrodes and a variety of physiologic measuring instruments are attached to an experimental subject and connected to a recording polygraph located in an adjoining room. The technician attending the polygraph can observe the physiologic recording as it is taking place and can communicate with the sleeping subject. The electroencephalogram (EEG, brain waves), electrooculogram (EOG, eye movements), and electromyogram (EMG, muscle activity, usually from a small muscle under the chin) indicate when a REM period is occurring by recording a combination of low-voltage, fast-pattern EEG, rapid eye movements, and the obliteration of skeletal muscle activity.

The first REM period of the night usually occurs after the subject has been asleep for 80 to 120 minutes. At that point, the technician can sound a buzzer to wake the patient and inquire about the patient's mental experience just before waking. In about 80 percent of REM awakenings, this conversation, which is recorded on audiotape, contains a description of a dream experience. When the dream scene is compared with the data recorded by the EOG, the direction of the eye movements can be observed to correspond with the dream scene described by the dreamer, to move as they would if the same scene and action were being tracked by the eyes of a waking person (Roffwarg et al. 1962). Except for the extraocular muscles, however, all the muscles of the body are relaxed during REM sleep. Although impulses to move in accordance with the dream experience are generated in the motor neurons of the cortex, they are inhibited from contracting the body muscles that would carry them out (Evarts 1960; Steriade 1984; Steriade and Hobson 1976). Occasional small ineffectual twitches do occur, however, and some observers have noted that these twitches are in muscle groups that correspond to the movement in the dream experience (Gardner and Grossman 1975). The dream experience is that of passive observer—it is safe to dream of doing forbidden or dangerous things, because nothing will or can really happen.

In contrast to the voluntary muscle relaxation, organ functions innervated by the autonomic nervous system are activated during REM. For example, heart rate, respiration, and blood pressure show a widened range of fluctuations and variability, as do skin and core body temperature and sweat gland activity. Penile erection occurs in males and engorgement of the clitoris in females. The EEG shows an activated, desynchronized pattern. Indeed, REM has been called *paradoxical* and *activated* sleep. Clearly brain and body are in a state of excitation and vigorous activation during dreaming sleep.

The account so far chronicles the physiologic changes that can be observed from the surface of the body in human subjects.* It remained, of course, for animal experiments to clarify details of the neurophysiologic changes and mechanisms of REM sleep.

THE PHYSIOLOGY OF THE DREAMING BRAIN

One of the most striking early findings made possible by the development of the microelectrode is that of David Hubel (1959, 1960a, 1960b), who found that neurons in the visual cortex increased their rate of firing when his experimental subjects (cats) went to sleep. This finding was confirmed and extended by Edward Evarts, who showed not only that visual cortex neurons increased their rate of discharge in REM to levels as high as those seen during waking visual activity but also that clusters of such activity could be observed at the same time that the eye movements were occurring.

The linkage of visual cortex neuronal activity with the eye

*The work of Hartmann (1967, 1973, 1982) and Hobson (1988) can be consulted for fuller descriptions of REM sleep phenomenology.

movements in REM can be interpreted in one of several alternative ways. J. Allen Hobson (1988) has suggested two possibilities. He notes first:

> The form of visual imagery during dreams is in part related to activation of an internal signal system within the brain, a system that operates during the wake state to keep track of the position of the eyes, and informs the visual centers of eye movement. And it is the specific signal properties of this internal bookkeeping system of the brain which may account for some of the distinctive aspects of visual experience during dreams. (p. 166)

The linkage of visual cortex neuronal activity also suggested to Hobson "the possibility that the activity in the visual sensory neurons was somehow a response to eye movement commands in the visual motor system" (p. 166). Alternatively, the linkage may, as I mentioned earlier, indicate that the eyes are reacting to what they are "seeing" in the dream, much as they would do if the dreamer were watching a movie or television screen. Yet another possibility is that the eye movements and the activity of the visual cortical neurons are simultaneous parallel but independent effects of a proximal common source of excitation.

This is an important issue. I do not know of any available neurophysiologic data that can fully resolve it at this time.* Some of the information about to be reviewed, however, may have some indirect bearing on it.

While many details of the neurophysiologic mechanisms and sequences involved are still uncertain, it is clear that REM is gener-

---

*Five neural control systems keep the eyes on target, all sharing the same motor effector pathway, the oculomotor nuclei of the brain stem. Two regions of the brain exert major influence on gaze by impinging on these motor neurons: the pontine gaze center of the reticular formation and the superior colliculus, which acts indirectly through the pons. Additionally, two cortical eye fields act on the premotor cells: the frontal and the occipital eye fields (Gouras 1981). All the above are infuenced by the ascending PGO waves, to be discussed later in this chapter. Exact time sequences have not to my knowledge been specified.

ated in the pontine brain stem, as was first demonstrated by Michel Jouvet (1962). Many brain stem structures and centers are involved in generating and terminating the REM phase of sleep, including aminergic structures—the locus coeruleus (LC), raphe nucleus, and peribrachial pons—and the giant cholinergic neurons of the gigantocellular tegmental field (GTF). Hobson refers to these structures acting together as a "Dream State Generator" (Hobson 1988; Hobson and McCarley 1977) and has proposed a model to explain how it works, the "Reciprocal-Interaction Model of REM-Sleep Generation." Some aspects of that model are controversial, but the controversial aspects are not directly germane to the issues to be discussed here. Because they do not compromise the generally accepted concept of a pontine "REM State Generator," I will use that term in the discussion that follows. "Dream State" should be understood to refer to a *brain* state (REM), not to a *mind* state (the dream, as experienced and recounted). Therefore this complex of brain stem structures is more properly called a "REM state generator."

This distinction will be important later in the discussion of another of Hobson's hypotheses, the "Activation-Synthesis Hypothesis of Dreaming," which does raise controversial issues directly germane to this work. But before discussing disagreements about theoretical interpretations, it will be best to continue reviewing the relevant information and commenting on questions raised by some of the findings, questions about inference and interpretations that bear on theoretical issues to be encountered later.

The REM period has two major aspects, a *tonic* aspect, continuously manifest in a fast, low-voltage EEG and in the inhibition of skeletal muscle tone, and a *phasic* aspect, intermittent ascending waves of excitation manifest as PGO spikes accompanied by bursts of rapid eye movements and increased firing rate of neurons in the visual cortex. It is this phasic excitation that is of the most immediate interest here. It bears directly on the questions of how dream imagery may be generated—and how it is ultimately to be understood.

PGO, THE VISUAL SYSTEM, AND THE DREAM STATE

PGO is shorthand for pons→lateral geniculate→occipital cortex, the ascending course of the waves of excitation that are started by the pontine REM state generator (see figure 8.1). Actually, it is something of a misnomer. The lateral geniculate is part of the thalamus—an important fact in that the excitation of the thalamus, which includes other sensory relay structures, has wider consequences than the geniculate alone. Many way stations in the thalamus are excited by the REM state generator. Although this discussion centers on the visual system, there are many "imageries" in the dream (visual, auditory, tactile, proprioceptive, and so on). For this reason some consider that it would have been clearer to refer to PGO as pons-thalamus-occipal cortex (PTO) or even pons-thalamus-cortex (PTC).

It has been demonstrated that firing rates of the cholinergic neurons in the gigantocellular tegmental field increase for as long as a second before the eye movements and PGO waves occur and also before desynchronization of the EEG (Hobson 1988). This interval would indicate that the giant cell firing cannot be caused by the eye movements or the PGO waves. The firing of the giant cells, then, constitutes at least part of the operation of the REM state generator. The excitation signals ascend to stimulate the brain stem nuclei that innervate the eye muscles that drive the rapid eye movements; the midbrain reticular formation, causing the general desynchronization of the cortex that is reflected in the EEG typical of REM sleep; and the thalamus, including the lateral geniculate body, which, as we saw, is the first way station for stimuli coming from the eye on their way to the occipital cortex, the primary visual cortex (area 17). It is generally assumed that the internally generated signals coming from the lateral geniculate in response to the PGO spike are conducted along the usual path to the visual cortex, where they are interpreted as if they came from the eye, because the occipital cells would have no way of knowing that they did not originate in the retina (that is, from outside).

139

FIGURE 8.1 Schematic diagram of the REM system. From the dorsal raphe nuclei and locus coeruleus (LC) to the gigantocellular tegmental field (TGF): (1) discharges from the LC usually inhibit discharges from the GTF during waking and NREM sleep; (2) the neurotransmitters involved in this inhibition appear to be aminergic; (3) this inhibition breaks down just before and during REM, liberating the GTF cells to discharge spikes. From the GTF via the lateral geniculate nucleus (LGN) to the occipital cortex (OC)—the PGO spike: (1) discharges from the GTF enter the LGN, a halfway station on the visual pathway from the retina to the OC; (2) via the LGN, these discharges then enter the OC, where they are apparently interpreted as coming from the retina; (3) because the pathway GTF→LGN→OC was the first one discovered, the discharges are called pontine-geniculate-occipital, or PGO, spikes. Other discharges from the GTF: The discharges from the GTF enter a multitude of other neuronal structures, apparently causing many of the typical phenomena related to REM sleep. Only two are outlined here: (1) discharges enter the oculomotor nuclei (OMN) and cause eye movements; (2) discharges enter the midbrain reticular formation (MRF) and cause general desynchronization of the cortex typical for REM sleep. Reprinted (with modifications) by permission from Hauri, P. (1977) The sleep disorders. In *Current Concepts,* 1st ed. Kalamazoo, MI: Upjohn Company (p. 15).

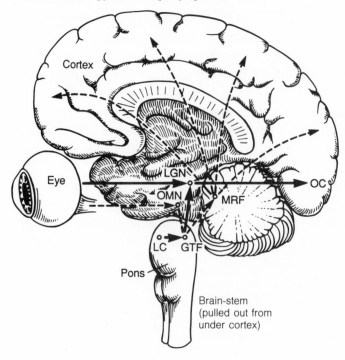

But visual perception is not that simple even in the waking state. A great deal of processing takes place between pattern registration in area 17 and conscious awareness of that pattern ("seeing" and recognizing a familiar face, for example). All the complex circuitry and processing in the cortical modules of the association cortex, area TE, and the subcortical circuits reviewed in the last chapter and this one have been called into play. Remember, a primate in whom area 17 is functionally isolated would probably be perceptually blind (Mountcastle 1978). Kandel (1981) postulates:

> To represent a familiar face or a landscape may require *parallel processing*, that is, activity in cells in different areas in the inferotemporal, peristriate, and striate cortices, with the cells in each area coding for a particular aspect of the stimulus. At this higher level of representation cells in many parallel visual areas are likely to be involved, and their simultaneous activity may serve as the feature detector.
>
> (p. 247)

HOW DREAM IMAGES MAY BE FORMED IN REM

The path from brain to mind is long and tortuous. The excitation carried up by the PGOs also spreads (via thalamic relays and midbrain reticular formation) to the entire forebrain cortex, including motor and visual association cortex.

The cellular columns of the forebrain association cortex, as well as area 17 and the limbic subcortical structures reviewed in chapter 7, constitute complex neural nets in which perceptual signals are somehow computed in preparation for conscious registration and for storage in memory. The retrieval process involves reactivation of processing patterns. These informational processing patterns may be stored as fragmented or part patterns of originally registered stimuli. They are ordinary residua of normal perception—different aspects of images separated for processing as they pass from lateral geniculate to area 17, and further separated as the information passes from area 17 through prestriate cortex to area TE in inferotemporal cortex (stage 2), where they are reassembled.

From there the incoming perceptual information is connected to limbic affect systems, which organize associations by connecting the new information to previously experienced stimulus patterns and link the various sensory modality aspects of each experience to one another. And the limbic elements (mainly the hippocampus) serve additionally as the portal of entry into memory storage systems.

The combined parallel-and-distributed, forebrain-cortical-subcortical neural networks must—somewhere, somehow—contain every last perceptual pattern fragment of perceptual information that has ever been stored. It seems to me that fragmented visual "trace" patterns might very well be particularly numerous in the stage 2 path of prestriate cortex, because many were formed there and presumably all passed through there at least once on the way to the final stages of perceptual and memory processing.

In the waking state all this perceptual memory processing takes place in the absence of PGOs. *Could this fact provide a clue to an explanation for the differences between imagery awake and imagery asleep?* That, after all, is one of the main target problems of this study. Let us, then, look at some of the differences.

First, in the waking state perceptual residua can be reassembled and visualized "in the mind's eye" but not hallucinated as in the dream (or in psychosis). It is interesting in this connection to note that Farah and her colleagues (1989), recording event-related potentials indicating local changes in cortical activity when subjects were asked to generate mental images of objects referred to by words they had just been shown, observed that the imagery "caused a slow, late positivity, maximal at the occipital and posterior temporal regions of the scalp, relative to the comparison condition, and consistent with the involvement of modality-specific visual cortex in mental imagery" (p. 302). Apparently the appropriate regions of the cortex are involved in waking mental imagery in "the mind's eye" even when the images are not misperceived as being "out there."

Second, in the waking state the parts are reassembled to provide a very close approximation of the original stimulus pattern. On the other hand, in dreaming sleep the brain is functioning in such a way that the parts may be rearranged and combined to form composite images, even from patterns that were originally registered on different occasions.

We know that in REM the neurons of the visual cortex are firing as actively as they do when the information is entering through the eye. More structures of the brain than just the primary visual cortex must be involved in generating the imagery of the dream, just as it is in waking vision. But—and this is the point I am leading up to—the imagery process in dreams may not be initiated in exactly the same way as in the waking state.

In waking vision, processing of retinal stimuli has already begun before the stimuli reach area 17, as we saw in chapter 6. Single cells in the retina are "on" or "off" cells; they are either excited or inhibited by light. Cells in the visual system respond to contrasts. From that elementary information, progressive abstractions that lead to the perception of lines, edges, shapes, motion, and so on are made possible by increasingly complex interconnections between cells and cell aggregates as the processing hierarchy is ascended. Although early processing begins even before area 17 is reached, continuous areas of the retina are still represented as continuous when the information gets there. Specialized cells in the retina, organized in receptive fields, connect via cells in the lateral geniculate to correspondingly arranged target neurons in area 17. The mosaic pattern of neuronal activity stimulated there reproduces the mosaic pattern or map of retinal stimulation initiated by the visual stimuli that fell upon it (Hubel 1988).

It does not seem likely to me that volleys of stimuli originating in a pontine "Dream State Generator" would be organized and patterned in anything like the complicated way that stimuli originating in the retina are. Therefore I think it unlikely that they would "look" anything like the patterned volleys of stimuli that originate in the retina. (I cannot find any data bearing on this point and cannot even imagine how it would be technically possible to acquire such data.) Would they not rather "look" like snow on the TV screen—unpatterned and random? That might be all that the busy cortical neurons of area 17 are "seeing" during REM. Why, then, don't dream images look like the image in a kaleidoscope or a brilliant, unpatterned computer graphics display? Why do they look like things we've seen before, or could have seen, or wish we'd never seen? We believe them and accept them as real in dream consciousness when we are in REM.

It may help to remember that a great deal of processing ordinarily occurs between the first arrival of information at area 17 and realization or awareness of a perception in consciousness. One explanation could be that stimulation of the association cortex by the PGO waves in REM activates perceptual patterns that have been stored in the neural networks there. Then ordinary stage 2 and 3 pattern-processing programs could proceed on from there to consciousness and be interpreted as though the stimuli reaching area 17 had just been made "from scratch" (that is, initiated in the retina). After all, the eyes are closed; nothing is coming in in the usual way. This explanation would imply that the primary visual cortex can be bypassed—one might say fooled. In this case, stimuli reaching it from the geniculate would be unnecessary or irrelevant during the dreaming brain state.

Another possibility is that PGO stimulation could activate stored perceptual residua in the association cortex and that these activated patterns would then follow a backward path through area TE and prestriate synapses, finally stimulating area 17 by a backdoor route, so to speak. Stimulation of area 17 by such a preprocessed stimulus pattern could then initiate ordinary forward-moving stage 3 and beyond programming into dream consciousness. The connections described in chapter 7 are all there, including synapses in prestriate cortex that relay impulses back toward area 17 (Friedman 1983; Friedman et al. 1986; Ungerleider and Desimone 1986).

The choice has to remain open. Again there is no empirical data to settle it. I prefer the second alternative, if for no other reason than that it seems to me to be closer to the way the brain may work. There is another reason, but I'll save that for later.

PART IV

THE INTERFACE
OF MIND AND BRAIN:
What Dream Imagery
Reveals

CHAPTER 9

Cabbages and Kings

"The time has come," the Walrus said,
"To talk of many things:
Of shoes—and ships—and sealing wax—
Of cabbages—and kings—
And why the sea is boiling hot—
And whether pigs have wings."
        —Lewis Carroll, "The Walrus and the Carpenter,"
              in *Through the Looking Glass*

"REMEMBER THIS!"

A Washcloth

Jim, a five-year-old boy whose mother is dying in the hospital, is home alone with his older sister. They have a fight; to chase her out of the room, he throws a wet washcloth at her. Running to get away, she crashes through a glass door panel, severs a major blood vessel in her arm, bleeds copiously, and is rushed to the emergency room just in time to save her life. *"Remember this!"*

After this incident, the father concludes that he cannot leave the children alone and sends them away to live in an institution. At age twenty-eight, early in the course of psychoanalytic work, Jim dreams: "I'm in a doctor's office, Dr. Riker. My friend Alfie walks in. I throw a pot at him and say 'Get out of here, you are supposed to be dead!' "

At the time of this dream the patient has been secretly involved in sexual behaviors that he feels sure would be considered psychotic, too "sick" for a psychoanalytic treatment. He is afraid to tell me for fear I will recommend that he be sent to a state hospital. His former friend Alfie, who had been involved with drugs (pot) and perverse sexual practices, had been committed to a state hospital with a diagnosis of schizophrenia.

A Grave

Carol's mother dies unexpectedly in childbirth when Carol is four and a half years old. The day before her mother's labor begins, the child in an angry argument kicks her mother in the abdomen and always thereafter feels responsible for her death.

At age eight, Carol is taken to the cemetery to visit her mother's grave. While standing there, she has the urge to urinate and is led to nearby stairs leading to an underground toilet. Sitting on the toilet, she touches the cold, damp concrete wall and thinks, "Mother is just on the other side of this wall. What if they buried her alive and she can't get out?" In a panic (heart pounding, perspiring, hands shaking, feeling as though she is being suffocated, she runs upstairs to the open air. *"Remember this!"*

Early in the course of psychoanalytic work, at age thirty-five, she dreams: "I am in a toilet stall. I try to leave but the lock on the door is stuck and *I can't get out.* My heart begins to pound, I am trembling all over, and feel like I'm suffocating." She awakens in a state of panic. The memory of visiting her mother's grave immediately comes to mind as she recounts the dream, and while the surface connection between the two is clear to us, our work does not penetrate into the deeper layers of her mind at that time. She then "forgets" all about the dream and our discussion.

At age forty-three, four years after termination of her psycho-analytic work, Carol boards a subway train at a station where the tracks are elevated, on her way to visit her aged grandmother, who raised her after her mother's death. The grandmother is in the hospital following surgical pinning of a fractured hip. The rest of the family wants to send her to nursing home, and Carol is upset: "They think it is time for her to die; *they* want her to die!"

After leaving the station, the train begins to descend into the subway tunnel. At the very moment that she sees and feels the descent below ground level, Carol experiences panic. Her heart pounds, she trembles, and she feels suffocated. At the first stop she leaves the train and rushes up the stairs, vowing never to go back down there again.

While listening to this story, I remember the visit to the grave, the early dream, and our first discussion of their relationship. I remind her, we discuss the connections again, and she understands, more thoroughly and deeply now than before. The subway phobia disappears, not to return.

A Bird

Eve at age five is upset about her mother's pregnancy and wishes for a baby of her own. Eve at age thirty-six is upset and conflicted about trying to become pregnant for the first time and has entered analysis. She has a dream in which a composite image appears, a collage of visual, proprioceptive, auditory, and physically painful perceptual residua:

> There was a man looking out of a high window. I wanted to get to him, but I was in the grasp of a large vulture and was being carried away. The claws hurt. The man's look implied "Just hold on—you can get

back to me." I was high up in the air; the vulture was holding me safe from falling, but it was also keeping me away from him. I woke up horrified.

In the analytic work, discussing the horror in the dream leads to her recounting a series of experiences beginning at age 5 when her mother was pregnant. In each of them she is horrified to experience the intensity of what she perceives as her mother's rageful disapproval and determination to prevent her (hold her back) from getting what she was wishing for at the time. Individual elements of the dream imagery are identifiable as parts of the scenery or of her bodily experience during those experiences.

A Book

The year is 1895; Sigmund Freud is working on a book, *The Interpretation of Dreams.* His intense ambition is invested in this work and is draining energy that could be going into more practical endeavors. He is defensive and guilty, feeling open to serious criticism—from himself and from family, friends, and mentors. He dreams:

> I had written a monograph on a certain plant. The book lay before me and I was at the moment turning over a folded coloured plate. Bound up in each copy there was a dried specimen of the plant, as though it had been taken from a herbarium.   (Freud 1900, p. 169)

His associations lead him back to a memory at the age of five when he and his sister were tearing (not turning) the pages from a book of colored plates and later could be further traced to a memory (age seven or eight) in which his father, annoyed with him for a boyish act that is usually regarded as an exhibitionistic display of ambition, declared, "The boy will come to nothing." *"Remember this!"*

Freud recognizes his wish for the book he is writing to be a masterpiece of historic importance. Then he can say, "You see, I did amount to something" (Freud 1900, p. 210).

A Diamond

The dream that follows is really about this book. I began the actual writing of the book during a fellowship at the Rockefeller Foundation Study and Conference Center, which is in Bellagio, on the shore of Lake Como, in Italy. Needless to say, years of preparatory study and work had already been done, and I was eager to start work immediately on arrival. But anticipation and daydreams had not—could not have—served as preparation for experiencing that first view of the lake framed by the soaring jagged rock faces and peaks of the Alps. I thought that seldom before had I been so exhilarated and felt so lucky and grateful. Stopped in my tracks, I didn't start work until the next day, when I woke up from a dream.

I was sure at first that the dream was not about the book. In the dream I saw sheer steep mountain cliffs, sparkling as though diamonds were scattered on the faces of the cliffs. I was reading about a major project to install many herds of goats on these almost perpendicular and virtually insurmountable rock faces. I should comment on the obvious, namely the intensity of my ambition connected with this writing project. I should note also that I am intimidated by mountains and seldom attempt a climb of more than a modest altitude. The mountains and rocks (Rockefeller?) in the dream could be negotiated only by mountain goats, certainly not by an ordinary human.

But was the dream not about the book? What about the word *reading*? I consider Thomas Mann's *The Magic Mountain* to be one of the greatest novels—and *The Interpretation of Dreams* one of the greatest books—I've ever read. And I hold both Mann and Freud in highest esteem as writers and as men of wisdom.

The diamond image entails a personal story from childhood. When I was eight or nine years old, I was taken to a renowned medical consultant in another city. In my presence he pronounced in grave tones that I had an obscure condition with a complicated Latin or Greek name. He referred us to a specialist in our home city for treatment. No explanation was offered to me. Being persistently curious, even then, I found my way to a medical textbook and located a disease that sounded like the one I'd heard pronounced. The text said that the condition was serious and perhaps incurable. *"Remember this!"* I wouldn't believe it. There had to be a magic cure (like the "cure" on the alpine slope in *The Magic Mountain*?).

It was during the depression. My parents could not afford the cost of a new treatment that had recently been developed and demonstrated to be effective. There seemed to be no hope after all. There were many worried family discussions and much distress until a practical plan was devised. My parents offered to give the physician my mother's diamond engagement ring as security, to keep in the event that they could not eventually pay him.

He accepted. The treatments were long and arduous but fully effective in time. And there was money to get the diamond ring back. I felt triply blessed and fortunate. *"Remember this!"*

But I seemed to have forgotten it when waking that morning. The dream *was* about the book, and when I thought about the dream, I was reminded of the experience, illustrating the putative function of what Freud called a typical "examination dream," a dream that serves to reassure the dreamer by saying, "You have been in an equally challenging and seemingly impossible situation before, and it worked out."

A CONCEPTUAL CHALLENGE

I'll try to remember that reassurance now since I'm confronting a task that does seem impossible: that is, to relate two disparate sets of data to each other. On the one hand there are five dream collages (and one phobia) put together using parts of visual, auditory, tactile, and proprioceptive percepts from different historical epochs of each dreamer's life, the dream images in each instance appearing to be associatively connected with each other by virtue of shared emotional meanings.

On the other hand there are 100 billion neurons in the brain (50 billion in the cerebral cortex)—each individual neuron with as many as 10,000 synapses—interconnected in neural networks that process information from within and without; cortical minicolumns containing about 260 neurons each, constituting the basic processing module; modules grouped in circuits, areas, structures, and systems according to functions, interconnected in such a way that individual cells, modules, and circuits of cortical and subcortical systems share operations by means of parallel and distributed processing, the entire array of neural network connections having been laid down according to genetic instructions and then modified (within limits) by epigenetic experience in a special way—"neural Darwinism"—that enables the individual animal to categorize environmental stimuli and to learn and remember those things it will need to know about its econiche to compete successfully and so survive to reproduce.

Awake or asleep, I see the task as impossible of satisfactory accomplishment at present, perhaps at any time. But there *are* ways to approach it. Many of the most gifted scientists of our time, from a variety of disciplines, have become sufficiently excited by the challenge to have switched their primary interests into the field and to have begun devoting their major energies to the behavioral and cognitive neurosciences and neurobiology. How can psychoanalytic psychology be fitted in? The asymmetry between clinical psychoanalytic observations and experimental neuroscientific observations is indeed imposing.

The contrast as drawn above was dramatized in this way to guard against any possible misunderstanding of what this book is

155

about—of what it does and what it does not (cannot) promise. It does not promise, or mean to assert, that there will be exact one-to-one fits between data from the realm of the mind and data from the realm of the brain. On the other hand, it *does* mean to assert that it is highly worthwhile to search for similarities and differences—and for roughly delineated isomorphisms—between functional patterns that can be inferred separately from data pertaining to each of the two domains. Despite the obvious asymmetry of the data, the two realms are more evenly balanced in respect to importance; each addresses different but equally important and complementary aspects of human life and experience.

Can study of perceptual memory processes as manifested in imagery during waking and dreaming states aid in developing a balanced understanding of mind/brain? The information reviewed in the preceding chapters should provide an opportunity to find out. The task at this juncture becomes one of explicating the logic of the inferences and interpretations involved in the theoretical formulations that will follow in chapter 11. Since their credibility depends on the soundness of that logic, I should first present an account of my reasoning in regard to conceptual problems that complicate interpretation of psychophysiologic data such as those reviewed here; that will be the task of chapter 10.

CHAPTER 10

Mind, Metaphor, and Brain

Confronting the Conceptual Challenge

Life acquires its own principles from the hierarchical structure of nature. As levels of complexity mount along the hierarchy of atom, molecule, gene, cell, tissue, organism, and population, new properties arise as results of interactions and interconnections emerging at each new level. A higher level cannot be fully explained by taking it apart into component elements and rendering their properties in the absence of these interactions. Thus, we need new, or "emergent," principles to encompass life's complexity; these principles are additional to, and consistent with, the physics and chemistry of atoms and molecules. —(Gould 1985, pp. 379–380)

The brain is a complex of widely and reciprocally interconnected systems. . . . The dynamic interplay of neural activity between and among these systems is the very essence of brain function. —(Mountcastle 1978, p. 7)

SOME CONCEPTUAL PROBLEMS: BLAZING A TRAIL
THROUGH QUICKSAND

Dreaming sleep is the state of mind/brain that should—if we ask the right questions—provide clues to some important answers. Toward the end of the last chapter, the task ahead looked all but impossible: to compare data sets of such different natures. Confronting it seemed like a nightmare—an "Impossible Dream." Still, we saw in chapter 8 that it was possible to make a good start by focusing on physiological and mental patterns of function in dreaming sleep and thinking about functional principles that can be inferred from them. But there are conceptual problems that complicate the process of working with correlational and comparative data. It would be well to explicate these problems before proceeding further, because any effort to formulate contemporary psychobiological models that account for information from both fields must take account of them.

These problems arise in connection with formulations that cross levels and domains. For example, it is tempting to postulate that similar functional principles govern certain aspects of memory function in both mind and brain. Nodal memory networks could be regarded as comparable to neural networks; associative links based on emotional meaning could be regarded as comparable to associative links based on connections between cortical neural networks and subcortical limbic, hypothalamic, and thalamic structures and networks. We are in fact headed in that direction. But things that sound alike are not necessarily alike, or the same. Could such an idea represent a mere semantic sleight of hand? There are two important conceptual problems to confront before we decide. The first is the problem of conceptualizing the nature of relationships between phenomena located within different domains. The second is the problem of conceptualizing the nature of relationships between phenomena located at different levels of functional and organizational complexity within the same domain.

158

And, as we shall see, the two may be compounded when they occur together.

In the end, the decision will have to be tentative, based on inference—available data are not sufficient for achieving reasonable certainty—and therefore subject to bias and to conflicting opinions. It is important, then, for the inferential reasoning to be as sound and explicit as possible.

Formulations Crossing Domains

The science of the mind and the science of the body deal with phenomena that occupy different domains. The former deals with motives and meanings, which have no physical qualities; the latter deals with matter and energy, which belong to the material realm. The disciplines on the two sides use different methods, concepts, and languages. Units are not interchangeable between the two realms.

One way to avoid or minimize this problem is to follow the dual-track approach described in chapter 2. That approach is based on the fact that logical and semantic devices such as models, metaphors, and similes are required to depict similarities between phenomena observed in separate domains; otherwise identities will be seen where in reality there are none, and phenomena detected in one domain may be mistakenly regarded as having been caused by covariant phenomena in the other.

Three steps are involved in following this approach. The first is to evaluate the data from each realm separately, in its own right. The second is to formulate on each side whatever functional principles can be derived from the data, in appropriate language and in forms compatible with principles already known and accepted in each of the respective fields. The third step is to examine the separately derived principles for possible formal and/or functional similarities, correspondences, or isomorphisms from which it may be possible to derive hypotheses and conceptual models that embrace observations from both realms, without mistaking resemblances for identities.

This approach, however, does not help in studying affects. Affective phenomena are manifested in mind/body changes that display virtually inseparable subjective mental aspects and objective bodily (autonomic, motor, and sensory) aspects. Emotions occupy both domains so coextensively as to embody the quintessence of the mind/body dilemma. This is both a problem and an opportunity, a fact that I did not fully appreciate in previous work (for example, Reiser 1984). This special circumstance warrants separate and fuller discussion, which will follow later in the chapter.

Formulations Crossing Levels of Function

Should what Mountcastle (1978) calls "the dynamic interplay of neural activity between and among these [reciprocally interconnected] systems" be regarded as taking place within an uninterrupted continuum from the simplest to the most complex level—that is, from the function of an individual cell to the function of complex circuits made up of many cells? Hardly. The interplay Mountcastle refers to is an interplay between systems of circuitry. And the individual circuits making up those systems represent different levels of complexity of structure, organization, and function within the brain (varying, for example, from relatively simple interactions of individual neurons within and between minicolumns of the cortex to relatively complex interactions between multiple cortical and subcortical circuits and structures such as those described in chapters 7 and 8).

This issue raises an often overlooked but critically important point: In biological systems, vertical shifts between levels of complexity are accompanied by changes in the nature of the functions encountered at the different levels (Blois 1988; Gould 1985). As one moves upwards, "emergent functions" are encountered: new functions that were not contained in the lower level "emerge" for the first time at the next higher one.

For example, a given number of neurons arranged at a higher level in complex parallel and distributed circuits can perform operations that the same number of neurons at a lower level, not so complexly arranged, are unable to perform. In other words, when appropriately organized, the whole can function as more than the sum of its parts. Operations at lower levels may not wholly explain or account for phenomena and functions that can be observed at higher levels. This fact can result in confusion, even conceptual error, when one is attempting to discern and define relationships between phenomena belonging to different levels, even within a single domain.

Consider the following illustration of the principles involved. It is relatively simple in that it involves a tiny upward shift in level and, as will be noted later, a correspondingly narrow gap between domains.

In the sea snail, *Aplysia californica,* the strength of synaptic transmission between neurons has been demonstrated to be dependent upon cell and molecular biological mechanisms (Kandel 1979). For example, increased influx of calcium ions through the calcium channels in the cell membranes of certain presynaptic neurons is associated with, and can account for, an increase in the amount of neurotransmitter released into synaptic clefts—and therefore the strength of synaptic transmission—when those neurons are stimulated (Kandel 1979). Conversely, decreased influx is associated with decrease in amount of neurotransmitter released into the synaptic cleft and with decreased strength of transmission. It can be concluded that strength of synaptic transmission is dependent upon the number of calcium ions that get into the neurons involved. There may be details to add concerning intervening steps in the mechanism, such as second messengers (Olds et al. 1989) and phosphorylating enzymes, but they still pertain to strength of synaptic transmission and are contained in the same functional stratum or a lower one, for example the molecular level.

These observations pertain to the level of cell function and of transmission of signals across the synapse. At the next higher level, however, that of synaptic *circuitry*, one encounters an emergent phenomenon when the snail responds aversively to an ordinarily neutral stimulus—the conditioned stimulus—when it is applied alone after having been repeatedly paired, in a specified time sequence, with a noxious stimulus—the unconditioned stimulus (Kandel et al. 1983). This new behavior, not fully encompassed in the lower cell and molecular levels, depends not only on cell and molecular mechanisms in the individual neurons involved but also on the pattern of their interconnections and prior experience. These new factors must be invoked for full explanation; a level has been ascended in the biological realm.

The Levels of Function in Brain and Mind

The neurobiologic mechanisms involved in memory can be studied at four levels of brain organization, and the research techniques and methods available and appropriate for investigating the relevant brain mechanisms vary according to the level being studied (Changeux and Konishi 1987). The levels are, from bottom to top:

Four Levels of Brain Function

Level 1: The Cell

Here the methods of study are those of cell and molecular biology, which illuminate the biological changes that occur in individual neurons while the organism is "remembering" (Kandel 1985; Kandel and Schwartz 1982; Olds et al. 1989). They answer "how" questions—for example, how is information stored?

Level 2: The Synapse

Here the methods are those of neurophysiology and of cell and molecular biology. Again Kandel's studies can serve as illustrations at this level. They also answer "how" questions by illuminating changes in the strength of synaptic transmission that occur while the organism is "remembering."

Level 3: Special Sense Systems and Circuitry

How does information from the environment get into the brain, and what are the structures and circuits that process it for perception, storage, and retrieval? Here the methods are those of the cognitive neurosciences, as exemplified by the work of Mishkin's program, described in detail in chapter 7. These studies answer "where" questions, such as "Where in the brain is the information processed?" They also answer "how" questions but at a different level: "How is information routed and processed at a systems circuitry level?"

It is taken for granted that individual cells and synapses in the circuits studied must be undergoing the changes identified by studies at the lower levels (cell and synapse), but mechanisms operating at these lower levels are not by themselves sufficient to answer the broader more encompassing questions of "what" is remembered or forgotten and "why." These involve level 4, that of neural networks.

Level 4: Neural Nets

Unlike levels 1, 2, and 3, which are all accessible to invasive techniques that allow direct manipulation of, and recording from, those discrete parts of the brain that are under study, level 4 has far too many cells and synapses to allow for direct manipulations and recordings. These are the almost unbelievably complex circuits that, as we saw in chapter 7, somehow manage to "get the visual information all together" after stages 1 and 2 have taken care of routing and organizing the information for perception and storage. David Hubel (1988) comments on the difficulties:

> To record from one cell alone and make sense of the results even in the striate cortex is not easy: it is hard even to imagine coming to terms with a cell that may be a member of a hundred constellations, each consisting of a thousand cells. Having tried to record from three cells simultaneously and understand what they are all doing in the animal's daily life, I can only admire the efforts of those who hope to build electrode arrays to record simultaneously from hundreds. (p. 221)

163

It is at this fourth level that computer modelling—"artificial intelligence"—is considered to offer the most appropriate and promising approach. Other strategies for investigating brain function at level 4 include brain imaging, such as Position Emission Tomography (PET) and Single Photon Emission Computed Tomography (SPECT) scanning, and Magnetic Resonance Imaging (MRI) and special forms of electroencephalography, such as the Power Spectrum EEG and magnetoencephalography. These techniques make it possible to correlate specified cognitive functions with levels of neural activity and local blood flow in specified brain regions. These methods are only now beginning to be used to investigate questions germane to the present work, but they hold promise for certain kinds of research in this area.

In the realm of mind, corresponding levels of complexity can be assigned to aspects of memory and other cognitive functions, as well as to methodologic approaches to their study.

Four Corresponding Levels of Mind Function

Level 1: Nonassociative learning
Level 2: Associative learning (Pavlovian and Skinnerian learning paradigms)
Level 3: Simpler forms of declarative (semantic) and operational (habit) memory
Level 4: Higher forms of declarative (episodic memory) plus symbolic function, language, and thought

For levels 1, 2, and 3 in the mental domain, the methods of experimental psychology, cognitive psychology, and cognitive neuropsychology are appropriate. For level 4, introspective methods like psychoanalysis are called for (figure 10.1). Accordingly, for higher cognitive functions like dream mentation, level 4 is the most appropriate level at which to seek correspondences across domains: neural networks on the brain side and nodal memory net-

FIGURE 10.1

LEVELS OF MEMORY PROCESS

NEUROBIOLOGY   PSYCHOLOGY

4. Cortical systems, circuits and neuronal networks	4. Symbolic processes declarative memory language
3. Special circuits	3. Procedural Memory
2. Synapse	2. Associative Learning
1. Cell	1. Non-associative learning

works on the mind side. (What levels of technology and conceptualization will be required to understand the functions of the human mind/brain that underlie the abilities to create, enjoy, and appreciate art, literature, and music? Will the search for the mind find all of it in the brain?)

Crossing Both Levels and Domains

If the problems that have been described obtain even within one domain, think how conceptually hazardous it could be to shift levels *and* to cross domains at the same time. The conceptual dangers of assigning causes and formulating explanations across levels and domains simultaneously are almost unavoidable, and in fact they abound in the literature about mind/brain topics such as those under discussion here.

To illustrate the problem, let us return to the relatively simple behavioral phenomenon of Pavlovian conditioning in the sea snail.

You will remember from the discussion above that a narrow but conceptually important level boundary (from synapse to circuitry) is crossed when the snail learns to respond aversively to a neutral stimulus. In addition, an equivalently small but nonetheless discrete domain boundary (from biology to behavior) is also crossed. In *Aplysia californica,* this latter boundary is so narrow as to be almost, but not absolutely, imperceptible. New words and concepts such as conditioning and associative learning must be introduced in order to describe and understand the phenomenon adequately. The psychological concept of learning as dependent on specified time relationships between events—time relationships that cause one stimulus to signify another—is not sufficiently accounted for by information about the biology of cell and synapse alone.

A question can legitimately be raised as to whether it is correct to speak of "mental" phenomena in such a simple organism. From an empirical perspective, it seems to me that we assign observational data about behavior in *Aplysia* to the mental realm by describing its actions, as we must, in terms that carry psychological connotations. Therefore I think it is correct, in this empirical sense, to think of mental phenomena (albeit rudimentary) in this animal.

With this simple animal example as background, imagine how interpretive problems can compound when we seek correspondences between observations in the human, not only from different domains but from different levels of complexity as well. For example, molecules are not ideas, and excitable neurons do not cause dream images—even though ideas ultimately depend upon molecular mechanisms, and dream images upon excitable neurons. The dreaming state of the brain (REM sleep) may be initiated by a pontine dream state generator, which involves cholinergic and aminergic neurotransmitter systems, but dreaming involves a different level of function, higher than pontine, and it is a phenomenon that belongs to a different domain, that is, mind. Conversely, wishes cannot cause REM sleep, which is a brain state, any more than a pontine REM state generator can cause a dream, which is a mind

166

state—in a different domain and at a higher level than the REM state generator.

If it is assumed, on the basis of such spurious reasoning, that the search for an answer to a fundamental mind/brain question has reached a point of closure, further serious inquiry into that question might cease—and that would indeed be unfortunate.

BUILDING A PSYCHOBIOLOGICAL MODEL OF DREAM PROCESS

It will not be easy to construct a theoretical model that will conform to the large and heterogeneous body of information available in both realms, but I am going to attempt it. The model will build upon the concept of the nodal memory network. The basic hypothetical premise, already anticipated, is that affective linkage, the main functional principle governing establishment and maintenance of associative links between sensory percepts in nodal memory networks (MIND), is analogous to the main functional principle by which neural networks govern development of associative links in the BRAIN. The premise has several aspects:

1. The MIND principle of affective linkage is analogous to the BRAIN principle of connection via limbic system-limbic linkage.
   a. Associative linkage in MIND is based upon associated percepts having been originally registered during life events in which the affect experienced was the same.
   b. Percept linkage in BRAIN is established by connecting newly registered percepts in sensory cortex with limbic affect centers that then pass those sensory percepts back to the association cortex for connection to percepts already stored in memory circuits there.
2. The MIND principle of nodal memory networks, which allows for condensation and displacement in cognitive process, is analogous to the BRAIN principle of neural networks, which allows for paral-

lel and distributed processing in computational information processing.

a. Perceptual residua are arrayed in MIND in nodal memory networks: networks of nodal percepts (percepts around which associated percepts cluster) interconnected by shared affect or affective potential.

b. Neural networks in the association cortex and subcortical limbic structures are interconnected in such a way that a single neuron may connect to many others in its own and neighboring, as well as distant, modules, and any one module may connect with many other modules and individual neurons.

While these inferred parallels between functional principles drawn from the two sides of the mind/brain divide are sketchy, they are empirically based, drawing on observations from clinical psychoanalysis and from cognitive neuroscience.

In reviewing data in the preceding chapters, I have emphasized features that started me thinking in this direction, but there is one further consideration that contributes to my feeling of confidence in developing the model to be proposed. It relates to the conceptual problems reviewed earlier in this chapter and to the emergence of a solution to one of them.

The problem of affect constituted a major stumbling block. The "dual track approach" calls for dealing separately with data from two domains. This method has been helpful in approaching other aspects of the mind/brain-body problem, but in this instance, it was limited by the fact that affect belongs to both realms. Observational data about emotions cannot be compartmentalized cleanly and dealt with separately, as can data about cognitive processes such as perception, for example. It is more difficult to separate the simultaneous subjectively experienced mental and physical aspects of an emotion than it is to separate the subjective experience of seeing an object from the simultaneous physiological processes in eyes and brain, which do not reach subjective awareness.

If you have ever had the experience of grappling with a problem for a long time and then coming upon an answer that you should have, or could have, been aware of all along but weren't, you know, too, the other part of it—having the sense that somehow you had known all along, without being aware of knowing. Something like that happened to me when I realized that the "affect problem" provided a promising opportunity for productive entry into the broader mind/body problem, the one it seemed to be complicating. The problem could be part of the solution.

In the early 1980s, I had diagrammed (and was thinking about) the mind/brain-body problem as being like two domains of information dealing with the same phenomena but expressed in different languages, units, and levels of conceptual abstraction (see figure 10.2). What seemed to be needed to integrate information from the two domains was a conceptual transducer or intermediate template that, like a Rosetta stone, could speak to both sides and, by translating between them, facilitate integrated understanding.

At the same time I was working toward integration of psychoanalytic with psychophysiologic information about anxiety: Comparing the phenomenon of signal anxiety in man with the Pavlovian conditioned responses in animals made it possible to regard signal anxiety in man as a modified version of the Pavlovian response to a conditioned sign of external danger, modified to serve as a response that would alert the person to the presence of an internal danger. For example, according to the psychoanalytic theory of signal anxiety, perception of an emerging dangerous impulse evokes a small automatic anxiety response. This physiologic response serves to signal the presence of the impending danger and activate psychological defense mechanisms to avert the emergence of the dangerous impulse into consciousness. In other words, the psychological defense mechanisms can be regarded as psychic equivalents of the animal's behavioral response of "fight or flight." Signal anxiety can be regarded as the physiological equivalent of the autonomic component of the animal's conditioned response (Reiser 1984, chapter 11).

FIGURE 10.2 A two-domain template. Reprinted with modifications, by permission, from Reiser, 1984, p. 18.

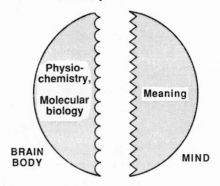

TEMPLATE

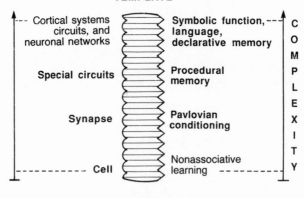

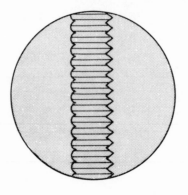

Also at the same time, I was formulating the concept of enduring nodal memory networks:

> Each of us carries somewhere within an enduring core network of stored memories—stored and linked in relation to a shared potential to evoke identical complexes of emotional experience. Such a network would be historically rooted in early and—for the child—cataclysmic events, either real or elaborated in fantasy. As development proceeds, the network would branch out with the occurrence of later events that set the earlier ones into resonance because they posed the same or similar problems. In this sense the later events could be thought of functionally as presenting emotional analogues or homologues of the earlier ones. Traces of such events and issues left encoded in memory then could be thought of as constituting *nodal* points as Freud conceived of them for the individual dream.   (Reiser 1984, p. 67)

Finally, in 1989, after studying and thinking about the information reviewed in the preceding chapters and after formulating the hypothesis about the parallel mental and physiological principles involving affect in perceptual memory processing in each of the two domains, I awoke to the realization that this complementary parallelism could be a reflection of the fact that anxiety, the prototypical affect, is a psychophysiological phenomenon and it is indeed in both realms. The theory of *signal anxiety* had been there under my nose all the time; it might well be an important part of the conceptual transducer I had been seeking.

The answer to the affect problem, then, was that affect, as a psychobiological phenomenon, would be expected to play a *single* role in crucial adaptive mechanisms such as those subserving perceptual memory—organismic mechanisms that display apparently different manifestations in the two domains but that stem from a common source.

neural memory
↑
organizing role of affect
↓
mental memory

These, then, are the personally exciting experiences and thoughts that contribute to my confidence in the probable validity of the concept of functional complementarity between nodal memory networks and neural memory networks. The concept conforms with the bulk of available information from psychoanalysis and cognitive neuroscience and is not seriously contradicted by any of those data. So I will "go for it," using that concept as a base upon which to construct a revised model of the dreaming process, a model that will take full and balanced account of currently available data from both constituent realms, mind and brain/body.

CHAPTER 11

Revising Dream Theory

The interpretation of dreams is the royal road to a knowledge of the unconscious activities of the mind.   —(Freud 1900, p. 608)

If it ain't broke, don't fix it; patches may do.

Virtually all the cognitive neuroscience reviewed in chapters 6, 7, 8, and 10 was unknown in 1900, when Freud published his dream theory, and this was still the case at the time of his death in 1939. Despite—or perhaps because of—the fact that he was first and always an empiricist and avid student of physiology and neurology, he chose to base the theory solely on empirical psychological observations, since no relevant physiology of the brain was then available. That he expected his theory to be explanatory in the psychological realm only must have been a disappointment to this "Biologist of the Mind," as Sulloway (1979) calls him, and we know from his writings that he anticipated the possibility that better explanations might be forthcoming from biology in the future.

This [confusion] is merely due to our being obliged to operate with the scientific terms, that is to say with the figurative language, peculiar to psychology (or, more precisely, to depth psychology). We could not otherwise describe the processes in question at all, and indeed we could not have become aware of them. The deficiencies in our description would probably vanish if we were already in a position to replace the psychological terms by physiological or chemical ones. . . . Biology is truly a land of unlimited possibilities. We may expect it to give us the most surprising information and we cannot guess what answers it will return in a few dozen years to the questions we have put to it.

(Freud 1920, p. 60)

Relevant physiology of the brain was not available then, but it is now. And some of it does not correspond exactly or readily with important aspects of Freud's theory. What does this mean, and what should be done about it? Does it mean that the theory is fatally flawed and should be dismissed as irrelevant and useless, of historical interest only? Or does it mean that psychoanalysis should hold onto the theory "as is," ignoring the new knowledge, confident that the theory is clinically useful and will probably turn out to be right in the end? Or does it mean that psychoanalysis is not a biological science after all, and that it should abandon any notion of being one, concentrating instead on its hermeneutic aspects and declaring itself to be a hermeneutic rather than a biologic discipline? Or does it mean that instead of throwing out dream theory, we must endeavor to revise it, taking into account observations and cogent ideas from psychoanalysis and cognitive neuroscience? This seems the most reasonable course to take.

TOWARD A BALANCED CONTEMPORARY PSYCHOBIOLOGICAL MODEL

This chapter will spell out in detail a hypothetical model of how the brain constructs a dream. Consideration of both psychoanalytic

174

and neurobiologic data will make it possible to propose a better-balanced contemporary model than would be possible using data from either side alone. The proposed model will be compared with Hobson and McCarley's model and in great detail with Freud's original model. Most of Freud's original modeling of mental operations, as we will see, was amazingly prescient.

Perhaps it will help to start with still another metaphor. The director of a repertory theater undertaking a new production can choose from a large but finite number of plays. Having chosen the play, the director then makes casting selections from a fixed number of regular, resident company players and, for special roles, from a larger but still limited "outside stable" of less frequently used players. For staging there is a store of props, scenery, and costumes that can be remodeled and otherwise modified to meet special needs and create special effects; there is a theater, with its lighting and sound equipment; and there is a crew of stagehands and technicians sufficiently familiar with all the above to bring off the actual production.

I have drawn this metaphor to clarify and underline what I mean by the concept of the nodal memory images in dreams. The dreamer, like the director, in selecting players and props and assembling them as elements in the production, is limited to the materials at hand: the dreamer's store of perceptual memory traces, the collected residua of his or her actual life experiences. In this metaphorical sense, the nodal memory images can be thought of as the "regulars"—the ones used frequently because of their capacity to portray many different roles. Their versatility would derive from their positions at junctions where many, often thematically different, associational threads connect with one another. In the staging of the dream, the facilities can be thought of as the functional capacities of mind/brain, capacities that enable the dreamer to store, arrange, rearrange, and retrieve memory elements according to—and in the context of—their shared emotional meanings, the music.

Before we leave the metaphor behind and go on to the dream itself, there is one thing more to note. The plays are ready-made. In a sense, each poses a problem or problems connected with the human condition and portrays an attempt to solve, resolve, or otherwise deal with them. The director's choice of play may depend on a variety of economic and artistic considerations, but the basis for the dreamer's choice is clear. According to the revised model to be proposed, the "dream-play" is staged by the dreamer because it is relevant to a current life problem and may portray his or her efforts to find a solution.

Freud noted that it is possible to reconstruct the ways in which the images of a particular manifest dream have been used and arranged so as to express, but not reveal, the latent meaning of the dream. He went on to note that the reverse is not possible: Even knowing a great deal about the dreamer—past life, current problems, cognitive and defensive styles, and so on—one could not possibly even guess what the dream would be like. To be able to predict it would, of course, considerably enhance the validity of his theory, which imputes meaning and purpose to the construction of the dream. The meaning, after all, is hypothesized to be related to thoughts that preceded the dream and to have participated in its construction. But the number of images and props and plots and players to choose from renders prediction impossible.

All the same, the issue is important, and even though we lack the ability to predict, it may be worthwhile, as an alternate strategy, to inquire into the process whereby the choices are determined. Are the choices random or lawful? If lawful, do they seem to have been made in order to express the meaning that can be discerned, albeit retrospectively? The answers could help us decide whether the meaning that can be discerned in the dream does or does not antedate it and did or did not influence the construction of the dream. It seems reasonable, then, in the attempt to model dream process, to start by thinking of dream formation as occurring in a series of stepwise sequences.

THE STEPS IN DREAM FORMATION

Step 1: Preprogramming the Dream

Psychoanalytic observations indicate that dream content can be related to current life problems that have been of sufficient concern to be on—at times in the front of—the dreamer's mind. Frequently the dreamer can recall having been preoccupied with them at times during the day of the dream. These observations may provide a clue as to when the process that will culminate in the dream has its beginning, namely during the day when the person's mind is being confronted by an important problem or problems.

From the psychoanalytic clinical observations, I hypothesize that feelings connected with current life problems and feelings from similar previous experiences that have been set into resonance by the current ones recruit and organize the associated images that will, during REM sleep, constitute the imagery of the dream. The day's residue in this scheme would be percepts, neutral in Freud's sense, that happened to register without special notice during periods of daytime concern about the life problems; these might be the first images to be drawn into the network of associated images that will be in the dream.

This hypothesis includes the premise that mnemic images in the mind are stored in nodal networks, arranged and held in place by affective associational connections—so called because the images are grouped by (and perhaps even arranged according to the strength of) their capacity to evoke, or potentially to evoke, the same feelings. In this way dream imagery is prepackaged during the day, not randomly but according to its affective associations, and prepared for activation when PGO waves come along during REM sleep. Examples of daytime concerns and the dreams whose images they recruited and organized: Freud's feelings during his meaningful conversation with Dr. Königstein and the the botanical monograph dream; Carol's phobic, panicky anticipation of marriage and possible pregnancy and the tannic acid dream; Jim's guilty concern about being sent away and the pot dream; Eve's conflicted, guilty intention to become pregnant and the vulture dream; my ambitious impatience to start work on this book and the diamond mountain dream.

I further hypothesize that the preparation for activation consequent to recruitment by feelings, as I have described, is accompanied by parallel lowering of excitability thresholds in those neural networks that, by virtue of having originally processed sensations originally registered during past experiences that generated the same or highly similar feelings, carry perceptual residues of these sensations. This hypothesis includes two additional cross-domain extrapolation premises: that there is an isomorphism between the mental functional principle of affective linkage and the brain functional principle of connection via the limbic system, spelled out in chapter 7, and that there is an isomorphism between the mental principle of strength of associative linkage (see chapter 5) and the brain principle of the excitability threshold. Although these extrapolative premises are in one sense cross-domain, in another they are not—that is, in the sense that affect belongs to and is part of both domains and is intimately involved in the mediating mechanisms in each of them, with signal affect serving as the intermediate template (see chapter 10).

Before going on to step 2, let us very briefly review the neurobiologic observations and functional principles that can be offered in support of these hypotheses, the neurobiologic connections and mechanisms that could mediate and make possible phenomena such as those postulated above. (Again, those readers who already have them clearly in mind or who may not be concerned about them might prefer to skip the review.)

Recall from chapters 6, 7, and 10 that neurons of the sensory and association cortex that store information are so arranged in neural nets that communication can occur between individual neurons, between modules within the same and different areas of cortex, and between all regions of sensory and association cortex and the medial temporal and limbic areas that process memory and emotion. In this way affectively toned associative connections are established between stored perceptual residua. Recall further that the brain communication circuits just described permit two-way flow of information, reentrance, and feedback, patterns that can be modeled in part by computer models such as parallel and distributed processing. The correspondence between the latter type of artificial intelligence systems and the cellular anatomical architecture and functional connections between cortical and subcortical systems in the brain is quite good.

Also important to recall in this connection is that information is transmitted from neuron to neuron not by point-to-point anatomical contact but across synapses traversed by the flow of chemical substances (neurotransmitters and neuromodulators). It is the action of these chemical messengers on the post-synaptic neurons that effects transfer of electrophysiological excitation—and thereby information—from one neuron to another. One of the major ways (probably the major one) by which experience modifies information transfer and ultimately behavior is by affecting the strength of synaptic transmission. In this partial neurophysiological description of "remembering" as it is manifested at the synapse between neurons, a point to emphasize is that resistance to or facilitation of transmission between neurons can be regarded as a fundamental biological aspect of memory. Remember also that the complex neuronal system connecting sensory and association cortex on the one hand with subcortical structures on the other hand is the system that is activated when the PGO wave reaches it.

Taking the information reviewed above as background, it seems reasonable to speculate that a condition of strengthened or facilitated transynaptic transmission within a memory circuit would manifest itself as a lowered excitatory threshold, favoring remembering; that the opposite—a condition of weakened transynaptic transmission—would be manifest as a raised excitatory threshold, favoring forgetting. Such a speculation rests on the assumption that there is a correspondence or isomorphism between the functional mental and brain principles involved.

Compare the *functional mental principle* underlying the arrangement of stored perceptual residua in nodal memory networks in which affective links connect constituent elements and influence associative strength with the *functional brain principle* underlying the arrangement of neurons in "neural networks," with synaptic links connecting constituent elements. (In the latter instance, the constituent elements are groups of neurons in perceptual processing circuits—neurons that have retained internal molecular changes, influencing the strength of synaptic transmission, as biological residues of previous conductances through those circuits [Kandel and Schwartz 1982].) The two functional principles do, in fact, appear to be isomorphic. In any event they seem to be sufficiently alike to permit the assumption that the processes they mediate in the separate domains of mind and brain could very well proceed in parallel.

Note should also be taken of the fact that information from both domains converges on the same structure, the hypothalamus, which is involved in both the biological motor (autonomic and neuroendocrine) and the cognitive subjective mental aspects of affect. Feelings, which, we have postulated, recruit memories in the mental domain, arise in connection with the cognitive processes involved in dealing with life problems. As the cognitive processes generate meanings, cortico-limbic circuits are activated, stimulating hypothalamic mechanisms that generate the motor aspects of anxiety (Reiser 1984).

The motor aspects in turn give rise to the sensory aspects and probably in part to the subjective aspect. At the same time, the hypothalamus, in response to the stimuli coming to it via the same cortico-limbic circuits mentioned above, releases centrally active neurohumors and stimulates peripheral endocrine secretions. These chemical substances participate in and modulate transmission of impulses across synapses. Here is a mechanism that *can* lead directly to altered excitatory thresholds in neural nets (that is, in the biological domain).

Taking the foregoing discussion into account, I conclude that the hypotheses offered earlier (pp. 167–168) are consistent with observations and derivative ideas from both realms and that it is reasonable to use them in constructing the model that I am proposing in this chapter.

Step 2: Activation and Development of the Dream Process

REM sleep is a manifestation of a unique brain state, unique with respect to both the mental phenomena and the physiological phenomena that accompany it. Step 2 is postulated to occur at night and to be initiated at the onset of REM. It is during the REM state that the dream process develops and the actual dream experience unfolds.

Before tracing the stepwise sequences that will be postulated to occur in step 2, it may be helpful to set an evolutionary perspective as a background (see also Roffwarg, Muzio, and Dement 1966; Winson 1985). In the revised model of dreaming under development here, I propose that the mind exploits the unique REM brain state for its own purposes, so to speak. This view accords prior biologic significance to the REM state. The assumption is that REM sleep appeared first in the course of evolutionary mammalian development and, favoring survival, was retained and further developed. The mental functions of the dream are viewed, then, as epiphenomena engrafted upon this basic brain state in the course of evolutionary development. As Stephen Jay Gould has described the process,

> Natural selection, as a historical process, can only work with material available . . . , the conventional designs evolved for ordinary life. The

181

resulting imperfections and odd solutions, cobbled together from parts on hand, record a process that unfolds in time from unsuited antecedents, not the work of a perfect architect creating *ab nihilo*.

(Gould 1985, p. 35)

. . . adaptations [are] contrivances jerry-rigged from parts available.

(Gould 1986, pp. 63–64)

I am suggesting that REM sleep was just such an available part. The anatomic/physiologic patterns of brain circuitry in the REM state of the brain, reviewed in chapter 8, are of such a nature that they can also subserve patterns and mechanisms of perceptual and memory processing that, also favoring survival, were retained and further developed and that acquired adaptive importance of their own. (This premise is similar to the view that language evolved as an epiphenomenon, physically dependent for its first spoken expression on the larynx. Speech exploits an anatomical/physiological apparatus (the glottis) that developed earlier to enable air-breathing mammals to swallow and breathe at the same time without drowning or choking to death from aspiration of ingested substances. I feel certain that this idea originated with Fred Snyder (1963, 1965, 1966) but have been unable to locate the exact bibliographic reference for it.

With this evolutionary perspective in mind, let us go back to step 2. The revised model postulates, first, that the excitation produced when the PGO spike reaches sensory and association cortex will activate first and most easily the neural circuits with relatively low excitatory thresholds. These would be the physiologic circuits recruited in step 1, because they include retained perceptual processing patterns originally used in processing sensory images registered during previously meaningful life experiences that involved emotions connected with the current life problem. For example, in Carol's tannic acid dream, the word *tan* was recruited from the episode of her brother's burn by current anxious, guilty feelings

182

about approaching marriage and pregnancy. The low-threshold neural circuit for re-creating the word *tan* would be the circuit that processed the sound of the word *tan* when she heard it as the first part of the word *tannic* during the burn episode. It would correspond to the portion of Carol's memory network that contained the memory of that episode. Another example can be seen in Freud's image of the dried plant "as if from the herbarium," recruited from the secondary school episode of the failed examination, by the current feelings of guilt and shame stirred up by the conversation with Dr. Königstein. In this example, the low-threshold circuit for re-creating the image of the dried plant would be the circuit that processed the image of that dried plant during the earlier episode when he failed to identify it correctly on an examination. It would correspond to the part of Freud's memory network that contained the memory of that episode.

Second, the revised model postulates that during the REM state of the brain, patterned impulses from such PGO-activated, low-threshold neural circuits, corresponding to perceptual images from meaningfully related experiences, would—as earlier suggested by Roffwarg, Muzio, and Dement (1966)—enter into and join the activated sensory processing cortical-subcortical circuits that somehow convert image-patterns generated by internal or external impulses into cognate experience in consciousness. (The routing circuitry has already been discussed in chapter 8, but the actual process of transducing neural impulses to cognate experience is unknown.)

In summary, the postulate states that the REM state of the brain provides neural mechanisms for stimulating associatively organized memory images, recruited by affect during the day, to "light up" and appear in the dream at night. Condensed in this way, the postulate seems simple, but that appearance is deceptive. As the preceding chapters indicate, the vast body of information and the detailed reasoning that led up to its formulation are far from simple. I realize that it must be flawed with respect to details, yet I feel confident that it is on the right track. It is consistent with available information in both domains, having taken both into account. And it provides tentative but reasonable first answers to some of the questions posed at the start of the book, particularly those pertaining to the images that appear in dreams and their relation to the thematic content. It has less direct bearing on the question of how the actual story line may be developed as the plot of the dream unfolds. We will consider that topic later in this chapter, when meaning is discussed.

Remember that the aim of this study in respect to dreams is to achieve a balanced contemporary psychobiological model of dream process. Freud's original model was taken as a point of departure. I myself was surprised to find how modest are the revisions needed to bring its provisions regarding imagery up to date in respect to contemporary cognitive neuroscience. The aim has not been to preserve that model unchanged as sacrosanct, and it has certainly not been to deal in any such way with psychoanalytic theory in general. The same reservation pertains to those aspects of the study that deal with perception, memory, and emotion, each of which is so inextricably involved in dream process. The focus has been on seeking a balanced contemporary psychobiological understanding, not on formulating an overarching general theory.

IMPLICATIONS OF THE POSTULATE FOR FREUD'S THEORY

The implications of the postulate are far from being as simple as the postulate itself. Discussing them poses a special problem for me, and it is only fair that I make it explicit, because it will, despite my best efforts, bias the discussion to some degree. Be forewarned: I have come to be impatient with, and sometimes irritated by, a currently fashionable trend to dismiss peremptorily (and I think prematurely) Freud's seminal and fundamental contributions to understanding dream phenomena and the dream process.

But as I have noted, there are aspects of his formulations that do not fit readily or easily with currently available neurobiological information. Still the decision to go for a revision of Freud's model rather than proposing an entirely new one reflects the best judgment I can make of the situation. The discussion that follows attempts to explain that judgment objectively. It takes for granted that readers have more than a casual acquaintance with the text of *The Interpretation of Dreams* (Freud 1990), particularly of chapter 7. Those who are not will either have to rely on my understanding or look for themselves. I know of no way to arrive at a responsible independent judgment about some of the more problematic issues without a reasonable understanding of that work. To those who have never read it, particularly those entering the field, I recommend a close study of it, not only for what is there to be learned but for the pleasures of reading one of the world's great books and of getting a firsthand glimpse into the process of discovery.

The implications of the postulate can be discussed with respect to two interrelated aspects of Freud's theory, the role played by wishes and the meaning of the dream. What is the role, if any, of wishes in the instigation of dreams? Is more than obvious meaning contained in dreams? In other words, does the manifest content conceal latent meanings, disguised for the purpose of censorship?

Wishes

Freud (1900) considered the dream to be the fulfillment of a "wish." Can it still be considered that wishes instigate dreams, when it is now recognized that REM sleep is started by a pontine REM state generator? We have already discussed the logical and semantic problems involved in that question; as we saw in chapter 10, they entail crossing both domains and levels. Biological events in the

brain stem are not wishes, and cortical-subcortical circuits represent higher emergent levels of brain function than do those in the
pons. Pontine events instigate the REM (dreaming) state of the
brain, but not the dreams. It is possible that wishes could cause
dreams, but not the REM state of the brain. In this sense we *can*
dismiss wishes as the instigators of REM, but not of dreams.

The evolutionary perspective of the proposed model will help
to explain further what I mean. It states that the mind exploits the
REM brain state for its own purposes, that the mental functions of
the dream are epiphenomena engrafted upon that basic brain state.
In the mental domain a wish is defined by Freud as "psychical
activity" that endeavors to generate a "perceptual identity," that is,
a perceptual experience that replicates or reproduces the perceived
sensations and images connected with the first satisfaction of the
body need giving rise to the wish. For example, if the infant is
hungry the wish is to reexperience the sensations of being at the
breast. I am postulating that this is exactly what the REM state of
the brain can make possible.

Let us go one step further. Wishes in Freud's theory are regarded as needs derived from "instincts"—another bad word
to some.

> If now we apply ourselves to considering mental life from a biological
> point of view, an "instinct" appears to us as a concept on the frontier
> between the mental and the somatic, as the psychical representative
> of the stimuli originating from within the organism and reaching the
> mind, as a measure of the demand made upon the mind for work in
> consequence of its connection with the body.
>
> (Freud 1915, pp. 121–122)

In other words, Freud considered that wishes were *mental*
derivatives of instincts, which in turn he considered to arise in
body tissues attendant to metabolic (biological) life processes. This
was at a time when he thought, in accordance with the physiology

of the time, that the brain was a passive organ in the sense that it did not generate its own energy and operated only when stimulated by energy from outside or elsewhere within the body. Instinctual energy would in this way stimulate and energize the brain to do the work demanded by body needs, such as for oxygen, food, water, and sex. Allen Hobson (1988) is quick to point out that we now know that the brain generates its own energy, and he therefore considers that Freud was wrong.

It is true that Freud was wrong, but only up to a point. The pontine generator does indeed supply the energic stimulus for REM, and therefore there is no need for the wish as instigator and ongoing energizer of the REM state. The brain has its own supply of energy to get it going. But does this really mean that body needs cannot stimulate the brain and lead to mentation in preparation for appropriate action? The answer is obvious: of course not. The brain may have its own fuel, so to speak, but it can be influenced in respect to what to do with it—where to go and why. And in sleep we know that bodily states may lead to dreams: thirst to dreams of drinking, hunger to dreams of eating, and lust to dreams of enjoying sex (so-called dreams of convenience). Remember that the whole body, as well as the brain, is activated in the REM state, particularly autonomic activity, as reflected in wide fluctuations of heart rate, blood pressure, respiration, and gastric activity, and in penile erection and clitoral engorgement. As Charles Fisher (Fisher, Gross, and Zuch 1965; Fisher et al. 1983) has pointed out, it is a state displaying ample indication of instinctual arousal. The REM state of the brain provides opportunity for reperceiving "experiences of satisfaction," Freud's (1900) formulation of the goal of a wish.

On the basis of these considerations, it seems reasonable to revise rather than dismiss and replace Freud's model, including the part about wishes. By adopting two minor amendments—(1) using terminology that clarifies domain and level confusions and (2) including an evolutionary view of dreaming as an evolved epiphenomenon—it can be brought into satisfactory conformity with contemporary cognitive neuroscience—so far, that is.

Meaning

The underlying issue with respect to meaning is that of disguised meaning—disguise for the purpose of concealment. Here, as I understand it, is the gist of Freud's theory as it bears on the question of meaning in dreams. It is not an exact summary; for purposes of clarification I have elaborated some of the denser passages and in so doing have undoubtedly added emphases and variations that may be more related to my ideas than his. That is the risk of a secondary text.

Freud assumed that conflicted instinct derivatives (for example, forbidden erotic, incestuous, murderous, or perverse impulses) present themselves to the mind as mental manifestations of needs to be gratified by wishes and that the mind, by virtue of being connected with the body, would somehow be obliged to gratify them. He pictured the mind as a hypothetical mental apparatus, a kind of optical instrument such as a telescope. External sensory stimuli come in at the perceptual sensory end, move forward into a memory zone composed of mnemic images lined up like a picket fence and strung out linearly as virtual optical images are in a telescope. From there the excitation progresses forward to the motor end, where appropriate response can be initiated. Freud assumed that the apparatus after stimulation would tend to discharge the excitation in motor action in order to return to its pre-stimulation level of excitation, according to "the (un)pleasure principle" which he derived from the "constancy principle" (Fechner 1889). This does not necessarily mean that the mind must return to complete rest. Freud visualized the memory images arranged so that the oldest and deepest memory images, those earliest registered, would be closest to the perceptual or viewing end of the instrument. (This will be an important consideration shortly.) Because the perceptual end is like a screen, perception consciousness serves both as a portal of entry into awareness and as a portal of entry into the apparatus for further processing. (Some stimuli may be too weak to enter conscious awareness but still strong enough to register subliminally and go on to further processing.)

In the awake state, Freud theorized, the current in the apparatus is progressive; it moves toward the motor end. In sleep, when the eyes are closed and the motor systems shut down, he hypothesized the current to be regressive, flowing in the opposite direction, toward the sensory end. The perception consciousness screen at that end can be excited on its inner surface by stimuli coming from inside the apparatus via this regressive current. If stimulated in this way from inside, it "sees" the pattern "out there" as if it came in through the eyes.

Freud postulated that body needs perturb—that is, set up excitation within—the apparatus, and depending on their nature and whether the person is awake or asleep (today we would say in REM sleep), that excitation can follow one of several paths. If a need/wish—for water, for example—is acceptable and occurs in the waking state, the excitation traverses the memory zone and the person will recall where and how to get water and rehearse the action (thought is experimental action). The program of action will then go forward to the motor end for implementation. If the need/wish is conflicted (forbidden or unacceptable), the mind's way out in waking states, when the current flow is progressive and the motor system accessible, is to deploy ego defenses to deflect and disguise it and to devise substitute actions to prevent the conflicted dangerous impulses from being carried out directly. (The result may be the formation of neurotic symptoms.)

In sleep, when motoric action is inhibited and the current flow is regressive, the mind's way out is to route the excitation in a backward direction to the perceptual end of the mental apparatus. There it can activate a mnemic image from the inside—a "remem-

189

bered experience of satisfaction," a dream image or hallucination. But even in sleep, becoming aware of the forbidden wishes and impulses in their raw form would be too upsetting and unacceptable. They would in that form wake the dreamer into a state of dysphoric anxiety, and the sleeper's wish to stay asleep is even stronger than the wish to be gratified. Therefore the mind exploits primary process mechanisms such as condensation and displacement to substitute and change images so as to disguise their true meaning and thereby smuggle them past the censor and at the same time establish a substitute perceptual experience. Visual images are particularly well suited to this process. Freud considered that dreams use visual images *because* of their capacity to represent thoughts without recognition ("Considerations of Representability"—recall the rebus example from chapter 2).

As the backward current of excitation travels toward the perceptual end (perception consciousness), it encounters and recruits associated (often fragmented) memory traces from earlier and earlier experiences, which are superimposed and rearranged, eventually registering as the bizarre, unreal, and unrecognizable sensory elements of the dream experience. (This is where the idea of the earliest recorded images being closest to the inner/deepest face of the perception consciousness screen is important to the theory.) As the current moves backward, the memory traces and thoughts they represent become increasingly primitive.

> If we regard the process of dreaming as a regression occurring in our hypothetical mental apparatus, we at once arrive at the explanation of the empirically established fact that all the logical relations belonging to the dream-thoughts disappear during the dream-activity or can only find expression with difficulty. . . . According to our schematic picture, these relations are contained not in the *first Mnem.* systems but in *later* ones; and in the case of regression they would necessarily lose any means of expression except in perceptual images. *In regression the fabric of the dream-thoughts is resolved into its raw material.*
>
> (Freud 1900, p. 543)

As I have speculated in chapters 7 and 8, I wonder if there could be, in REM sleep, an actual current in the brain that corresponds to this part of Freud's hypothetical model—that is, a regressive current activating early perceptual traces situated just inside the perceptual screen. Under PGO activation, excitation would thus spread from area TE in a backward direction to area 17, thereby activating perceptual residues just inside area 17 and stimulating visual neurons there.

There are two additional suggested revisions to Freud's model to add here. First, I suggest that the memory zone of the apparatus be considered to consist of nodal memory networks rather than linearly arrayed mnemic images, but still arranged in a historically regressive direction with the earliest and deepest traces closest to the perceptual end. Second, I believe that activation of sensory and association cortex by ascending excitation from the pontine REM state centers should be regarded as supplying the basic energy for the neural processes underlying the mental characteristics of dreaming, the processes that led Freud to postulate regressive current in the mental apparatus and a requirement for instinctually derived energy in order for mnemic traces to reach sufficient intensity to produce the dream hallucinations. The functional principles of his *mental* model are, as I have tried to show, just as well served by the more recently discovered neural information, and therefore, in my opinion, they still have heuristic explanatory value with regard to the observed mental characteristics of dreams.

Freud considered that the rebuslike dream images depict "intermediate dream thoughts"—thoughts generated in an attempt to deal with current conflicts involved in meaningful life experiences of the day. These intermediate thoughts in turn were postulated to connect with past "repressed" conflicts that remain unresolved but active in the mind. The dream work, he said, disguised the meanings encompassed by these conflicts—the "latent content"—by using mental mechanisms to convert it into the "manifest content." His interpretive technique consisted of asking the dreamer to "free associate" to these dream images, in the expectation that the associations would undo the dream work by tracing the associative paths back to the relevant but forgotten historical events.

A final aspect of the dream work is what Freud called "secondary revision." In remembering and recounting the dream, the dreamer revises it to make a more intelligible and acceptable narrative, as a good editor does with a somewhat garbled manuscript. Freud considered this aspect a less basic but still important part of the dream work.

As postulated earlier, the dream unfolds and develops in step 2 during REM sleep, the main images having been recruited by affect during the day to appear later during REM sleep. It is probable that the narrative action itself also develops in REM; episodic memories of events (Tulving 1989) can be recruited along with the images that were registered during those events. The events, while connected with past (often unresolved) life situations that generated emotional problems similar or identical to those the person is currently facing, would most likely be disconnected from each other in time and circumstances, and the process of "secondary revision" would be helpful in organizing them into credible narrative sequences or story lines.

Allen Hobson and Robert McCarley (1977) and Hobson (1988), however, regard this editing and rationalizing function to be the *major* and most important mental work connected with the dream. They assert that in the activation of forebrain, ascending tonic and phasic (PGO spike) stimuli play randomly across the entire sensory and association cortex, lighting up whatever stored images happen to be in their path. They consider this random activation to account for the bizarre, often grotesque imagery and apparently nonsensical content of the dream experience. The main and only mental contributions, they say, come in the cognitive operations of trying to make a sensible narrative. According to Hobson (1988), whatever meanings can be discerned are apparent immediately. Inquiry with the dreamer into the significance of the dream images and events produces answers that reveal the person's cognitive style, and these afterthoughts may point to issues of current concern. Therefore, according to this view, inquiry and discussion are clinically useful in much the same way as inquiry into responses to projective psychological test stimuli such as the Rorschach or Thematic Apperception Test would be.

This model, which Hobson and McCarley call the activation-synthesis hypothesus, has several immediately apparent shortcomings, in my view. First, if the imagery were indeed generated in such a random fashion, how would repetitive dreams be explained? The revised model proposed in this book is strongly supported by the phenomenon of repetitive dreams, especially those occurring in individuals suffering from severe emotional trauma, as in war experiences (Post-Traumatic Stress Syndrome), natural disasters, and other catastrophic experiences. In those instances the identical scenes, action, and overwhelming feelings of horror and terror occur over and over again in repetitive nightmares. Surely these repeated dreams are rigidly preprogrammed and could hardly be explained by random stimulation of the frontal cortex.

Second, the model would not very well explain the clear and obvious relation of dream themes to current life problems. This close relationship is more frequently and regularly observed than would be expected if the dream were as randomly generated as the activation-synthesis model suggests.

Moreover, studies of deep medial temporal lobe structures reveal that electrical stimulation in the region of these structures may induce vivid dreamlike recall of earlier complex life experiences, including imagery that is sometimes intense enough to be hallucinatory (Ferguson et al. 1969; Mahl et al. 1964; Penfield and Jasper 1954; Penfield and Perot 1963). This finding would seem to indicate again that the neural memory systems can contain complicated and meaningfully organized scenarios for recall under appropriate conditions.

Finally, it seems to me that one could hold such a view as the activation-synthesis model only by ignoring the weight of clinical data such as that reviewed in chapter 5 and by failing to take into account the cognitive neuroscience data reviewed in chapters 6 and 7, which indicate that processing of sensory stimuli is far more organized and orderly than this model acknowledges. In my view the activation-synthesis model assigns too much explanatory importance to the pontine REM state generator and too little to higher-level mind/brain processes. It is an approach mainly from the bottom up. But in overlooking what may be learned from a top-down approach, it ends up with an unbalanced view. It is better, I think, to consider the view from both directions, as did Howard Roffwarg, Joseph Muzio, and William Dement (1966), for example, in pondering the significance of the REMs of neonates:

> The REM's of neonates, which likely have no counterpart in patterned vision, are extraordinarily similar to those of sleeping adults (though they are somewhat more clustered and vertical). In view of this fact, we wonder whether the eventual development of dream imagery may involve a process by which the cortex "fits" sensory images to discharge patterns of brainstem origin established before the accumulation of sensory experience. The cortex may develop some modulating influence over these pontine discharges, but the basic discharge rhythm probably has a brainstem genesis. In this sense, the dream would truly appear to be born in the brainstem but clothed in the cortex. (p. 13)

EVOLUTIONARY CONSIDERATIONS

This quotation leads quite naturally into the last issue that remains to be discussed, that is, the implications of the evolutionary perspective for understanding the dream process. There are two main hypotheses concerning the possible biological significance of REM sleep in respect to mammalian evolution, hypotheses that bear on the topic of the dream. The first is represented in the quotation above. Roffwarg, Muzio, and Dement (1966) postulated that the

REM state, in providing excitation of higher brain centers during sleep, may serve to maintain the central nervous system in a state of readiness to react to exigencies of the real world—for example, the approach of a predator while the animal is asleep. Having demonstrated that there is more REM sleep in infancy and early childhood than in adulthood, they also hypothesized that the REM mechanism provides endogenous stimulation to higher brain centers in early stages of development, during developmental epochs when such stimulation would be crucial in assisting structural maturation and differentiation of key motor and sensory systems. In other words, REM would serve as a stimulating nutrient for the immature, developing nervous system in neonatal life. (We know now that this hypothesis can be extended to phases of intrauterine life; REM has been demonstrated to occur in the fetus [Birnholz 1983; Parmelee et al. 1967].)

The survival advantage that such effects would provide for the species in natural selection is self-evident. And, as the quotation implies, the REM mechanism, although evolved for different reasons, would also have provided a way for the cortex to "fit" sensory images to discharge patterns of brain stem origin. It is this latter aspect of the mechanism that I postulate was taken over and exploited in the service of accomplishing important mental tasks such as cognitive problem solving.

The second evolutionary hypothesis is that of Jonathan Winson (1985), which assigns REM a crucial role in memory processing. Winson postulates that in the course of evolution mammals, in order to survive, had to develop a way of taking in new information and connecting it with memories of past experiences in order to formulate plans for adaptive behavior during the waking state—a way that would not depend on adding additional cortical tissue. As he points out, "should the organization of man's brain have been similar to the echidna, he might have needed a wheelbarrow to carry it around. In short, man would not have evolved" (p. 206).

Winson goes on to propose the following hypothesis:

What was the scheme that nature hit upon in marsupial and placental mammals? I propose that it was, in computer terms, off-line processing. (Off-line processing is the acquisition of input information and its temporary storage in computer memory until a time when processing components are available.) The task of associating recent events to past memories and evolving a neural substrate to guide future behavior was accomplished when the animal was asleep. A small prefrontal cortex was sufficient because it did not have to work on this task of integration simultaneously with the processing of new information—it could perform its integrative function in a more leisurely manner during sleep. The new stage of sleep, REM sleep, was the crucial element (although not the whole story). (pp. 206–207)

Winson locates the crucial mechanism in the hippocampus, which is the central structure in the limbic system that is intimately associated with memory (see chapter 7). Theta rhythm, a brain rhythm that occurs during processing of sensory information (Winson 1985), occurs during REM sleep, and Winson has obtained in his laboratory theta rhythm data that suggest REM sleep processing of information (Winson 1985, p. 208). These findings, along with other data he cites, lead him to the postulate that "dreams are a window on the neural process whereby, from early childhood on, strategies for behavior are being set down, modified, or consulted" (1985, p. 209).

In REM, theta rhythm appears to be passing through the circuitry connecting the entorrhinal cortex, the trisynaptic circuit of the hippocampus, the prefrontal cortex, the thalamus, the amygdala, and the primary sensory receiving areas of the frontal cortex and driving (or otherwise influencing) its activity. This is the circuitry involved in routing perceptual input to its final destination in frontal cortex, in laying down affectively toned associations, and in consolidating the information into long-term memory by the process of long-term potentiation (LTP) in the hippocampus. All of this suggests that during sleep—perhaps especially during REM sleep—the hippocampus may be actively involved in processing the perceptual input of the day, sorting out, saving, and filing what is important and discarding what will not be needed (Winson 1985).

Some such processes would be necessary for two reasons. First, there is not enough space to store everything that comes in during the course of a lifetime, and second, the apparatus probably has to be cleared nightly to make room for the fresh perceptions that will come along the next day (Crick and Mitchison 1983). Sleep would be an ideal time, since perceptual input then is at a minimum and the circuits that would be busy during waking hours would be open and available for off-line processing.

In other words, REM sleep may provide a mechanism for memory processing whereby the voluminous informational input of the day may be sorted at leisure during sleep, when the circuits are not otherwise busy. It seems reasonable to me to expect that the hippocampal sorting and filing would be carried out in correspondence with the original input processing route and the connections established along the way and that the areas and circuits of the cortex that are activated when the PGO arrives would be predetermined or preconfigured in a corresponding way, similar to the way in which, as has been postulated, the perceptual residua in the mental sphere could be preconfigured by affect.

If such were the case, affective connections would exert considerable influence on those neural sorting and filing operations, and the sense we can make of dreams through the psychoanalytic process would reflect the influence of those affective connections as they manifest themselves in both domains. The mental memory process would consist of deciding which percepts to store and which to discard, on the basis of their relation or lack of relation to significant events already in memory, as Stanley Palombo (1973, 1978) had suggested earlier on the basis of psychoanalytic-dream laboratory studies. From an evolutionary and adaptational perspective, I would understand this concept to mean that the REM mechanism, first developed to store information relating to activities important for physical survival, could subsequently have

197

evolved in humans into a mechanism for psychological survival, as the psychosocial environment became increasingly complex. This mechanism too would have provided an obvious advantage in natural selection over the course of time.

Winson's idea that the dream experience may reflect these purposive off-line memory processing functions may help in understanding how the subjective perceptual aspect of the dream experience develops. The dream imagery could represent the printout in dream consciousness generated by these underlying neural events.

CONCLUSION

In this chapter several additive revisions have been suggested for the purpose of bringing Freud's model of dreaming into conformity with—and reflective of—available information from the fields of cognitive neuroscience and psychoanalysis. The suggested revisions include the following:

1. An evolutionary perspective is added, which considers that the mind exploits the unique REM brain state for its own cognitive purposes, including problem solving and related memory functions.
2. The dream process is postulated to start with daytime problem-solving concerns (step 1). These daytime experiences generate feelings that in turn serve to recruit mnemic image patterns from the nodal memory networks, which supply the images that appear in the dream when the REM state and PGO spikes occur. The day's residue in this scheme would be percepts (neutral in Freud's sense) that happened to register without special notice during periods of daytime concern about the problems.
3. It is postulated that the unique physiology of the REM brain state provides neural mechanisms for activating the associatively organized mnemic perceptual image patterns (recruited by affect in step 1) to "light up" (appear) in the dream and develop into dream events. Activation of the sensory and association cortex by ascend-

ing excitation from pontine REM state centers may be regarded as supplying the basic energy for the neural processes underlying the mental characteristics of dreaming that led Freud to postulate a "regressive current" and a requirement for instinctually derived energy to produce dream hallucinations. This substitution does not interfere with the heuristic explanatory value of the functional mental principles in Freud's model as regards the observed mental characteristics of dreams.

4. A nodal memory network pattern is substituted for the linear arrangements in the memory zone of Freud's hypothetical mental apparatus.

If the distinction between REM as a brain state and the dream as a mental product is kept in mind, these revisions do not necessitate any fundamental alteration of Freud's views regarding the dream as the "fulfillment of a wish" and "a royal road to a knowledge of the unconscious activities of the mind." Note that activities includes mechanisms as well as content and that a royal road does not mean the only road.

Are these really to be regarded as minor revisions? Certainly they are neither few nor trivial. They are important and necessary in order to bring the model into balanced conformity with contemporary cognitive neuroscience and psychoanalysis. In this sense they are major additive revisions; they are minor only in the sense that they do not require major modification of the functional mental principles originally formulated by Freud without the advantage of the currently available information that creates the need for them. I have already stated my bias (pp. 184–85). Whether they are regarded as major or minor is a matter of personal judgment and preference. It does not influence the facts one way or the other, and so is of little real moment. On the other hand, the questions next to be addressed are of real moment.

Is the resultant modified model a complete one? Is it accessible to validation or disproof by currently available empirical methods? The answer to both of these important questions is, of course, no.

We knew from the start that affirmative answers to these questions would be far beyond the reach of this study. The goal rather has been to evaluate the fit of the postulated mental mechanisms with cognitive neuroscience and with psychoanalytic observations, thereby to achieve a balanced contemporary psychobiological model of the dream process. I think that that goal has been achieved. We have accomplished what we set out to do. The modified or revised model does make it possible to formulate a new psychobiological view of the dream process that is both balanced and contemporary—a view that would not have been visible from either side alone. *Dreaming in man can be defined as the subjective experience of vital memory and problem-solving cognitive functions, made possible by the special psychophysiological conditions that obtain in mind/brain-body during REM sleep.*

Epilogue: Another Dream

This book stands as an example of both the promise and the limitations of one individual effort—as competent as could be expected under current conditions—to deal in depth with one selected sector of mind/brain function. To the extent that it succeeds, it does so mainly by raising questions and providing hints—no more—in the direction of solutions. It is not enough.

The idea of understanding mind exclusively in terms of brain function represents a distant and perhaps impossible dream. The best that the empirical sciences of mind and brain can achieve at present is the formulation of conceptual approximations. Optimally, such formulations should be based on observable facts and should take appreciative cognizance of similarities and differences in methods and observations that obtain in each of the two domains. In effect, this means that such integrations as can be attained will occur in individual, prepared minds, minds of persons who in one way or another have achieved a capacity as well as motivation for it.

Not many such, you say? Who knows? I suspect that there are many more than we realize but that they are scattered in widely distributed and often unexpected places and don't often communicate about such esoteric matters with one another or publish about them. There are, of course, outstanding and well-known exceptions in the brain and cognitive neurosciences: Jean-Pierre Changeux, Gerald Edelman, Michael Gazzaniga, Eric Kandel, Mortimer Mishkin, Karl Pribram, Steven Rose, and Jonathan Winson, to name a few whose breadth of interest has represented a source of personal inspiration for me. I also know many younger neurobiologists and cognitive neuroscientists who share the same interests and potential. And there will be still more to follow. But—and here is the main point—their potential for increasing our conceptual understanding of mind/brain may be not be fully realized, and that is too bad. I think it could be realized without seriously diverting them from their primary work, which is mainly, sometimes exclusively, focused on the brain.

The same is true on the other side of the "Great Divide." Many psychoanalysts, beginning with Freud, have focused intense interest on mind/brain-body: Franz Alexander, Michael Baasch, Theresa Benedek, George Daniels, Felix Deutsch, Marshall Edelson, George Engel, Charles Fisher, Merton Gill, Peter Knapp, Maurice Levine, Joseph Lichtenberg, Karl Menninger, Arthur Mirsky, Milton Rosenbaum, and Herbert Weiner, to name only a few. And there are many younger psychoanalysts (and more will follow) with the same interests and potential, but I fear that their potential too for increasing our conceptual understanding of mind/brain may not be fully realized. Again, I think it could be, without seriously diverting them from their primary work, which is mainly, sometimes exclusively, focused on the mind.

Why should we worry about this failure? For several reasons. First, the very same explosion of scientific knowledge and technological progress that has in so many ways improved the opportunity for physical health in life has also contributed to serious deterioration of the prospects for continuing existence on this planet. Second, the functioning of human beings, both in health and in disease, reflects the interaction of biological, psychological, and social forces and mechanisms. Human behavior—and the human condition—can be fully understood only by taking all three into consideration. If we do not know as much as we potentially could about how the mind/brain functions to sustain physical and mental health and to guide human behavior, we should worry. We need all the help we can get.

Throughout the course of writing this book, I repeatedly experienced the frustration of wanting to develop and suggest practical ideas for experiments that might bring psychoanalysis and cognitive neuroscience closer to conceptual convergence. I did think of some but realized that they could not get past the armchair stage without access to interdisciplinary collaborators and facilities that are currently unavailable. Those few who could collaborate are not, as I will explain shortly, free to do so, nor are all of them as ideally prepared for it as might be wished.

This is not to say that there are no productive research programs involving psychoanalysis and other behavioral sciences. Several examples were cited in chapter 4. Another example that is particularly cogent to the development of bridges between psychoanalysis and neuroscience is the work of Howard Shevrin (1978, 1988; Shevrin and Dickman 1980). He has succeeded in establishing the beginnings of meaningful correlations between mental data indicative of unconscious conflict and particular configurations of evoked sensory brain potentials. But such examples are exceptions. And the investigators are people who somehow prepared on their own, rather than in training programs designed to prepare scientists for this particularly demanding type of work.

Ideally, to be creative in interdisciplinary research, a person should be educated in two disciplines in order to work in one and collaborate with the other. The desirability of such an education is particularly true in the case of psychoanalysis and neurobiology, but it would also obtain across other disciplinary boundaries, whenever training in each of two sentient disciplines is too specialized to allow for the degree of understanding of the methods, data, and concepts of the other required for meaningful collaboration and conceptual convergence. New patterns of training would have to be established for such collaboration—not for all trainees but for some who would be selected for it on the basis of special interest and promise.

The university should be at the center of efforts to help. It not only should, it would—if it could! Only universities could embrace the full range of disciplines that would be involved in seeking integrations across the multiple interfaces that could be involved: molecular genetics, molecular biology, cell biology, neurophysiology, neuroanatomy, neurochemistry, neuropsychopharmacology, all branches of psychology, including psychoanalysis, computer science, sociology, anthropology, earth sciences, political science, history, and the humanities. (Remember, this is a dream.)

But even then each scientist in training in two disciplines would require special additional support for the extra time and relatively slower productivity the dual training would entail. And provision would have to be made for survival in the academic "publish or perish" marathon and for a viable financial career in the scientist's primary discipline or profession. Ideally, physical facilities would be needed to house institutes where the training and research could be carried out in surroundings providing for proximity and communication between faculty and trainees.

Universities would require financial aid in substantial amounts. Of course this is a dream for the future, and I realize that the problems listed above are wider than would be encompassed by solving mind/brain problems alone. But can we afford not to try? Can we afford to delay? Would the costs be supported by private foundations, and/or by industry, and/or by government? Is anybody out there?

As I wrote the book, a more modest dream was that one or two enterprising young investigators who are equipped to do so (by whatever means) might be inspired to pursue one or two of the questions raised. I still entertain that wish and would be happy for it to come true, but I am sad to think that it might not.

References

AMACHER, P. (1965) *Freud's neurological education and its influence on psychoanalytic theory.* Psychological Issues, Monograph 16. New York: International Universities Press.

ASTON-JONES, G., AND BLOOM, F. E. (1981) Norepinephrine-containing locus coeruleus neurons in behaving rats exhibit pronounced responses to non-noxious environmental stimuli. *The Journal of Neuroscience* 1:887–900.

ASTON-JONES, G., FOOTE, F. L., AND BLOOM, F. E. (1984) Anatomy and physiology of locus coeruleus neurons: Functional implications. In *Norepinephrine: Clinical Aspects,* ed. M. G. Ziegler and C. R. Lake. Baltimore: Williams & Wilkins.

BIRNHOLZ, J. (1983) The development of human fetal learning. *Science* 222:516–18.

BLOIS, M. S. (1988) Medicine and the nature of vertical reasoning. *The New England Journal of Medicine* 318:847–51.

BONIN, G. VON, AND BAILEY, P. (1947) *The Neocortex of Macaca Mulatta.* Urbana: University of Illinois Press.

CARTWRIGHT, R. D. (1977) *Night Life.* Englewood Cliffs, NJ: Prentice-Hall.

CHANGEUX, J.-P., AND KONISHI, M. (1987) Introduction. In *The Neural and Molecular Bases of Learning.* Chichester: John Wiley & Sons.

CRICK, F., AND MITCHISON, G. (1983) The function of dream sleep. *Nature* 304:111–14.

DAHL, H., TELLER, V., MOSS, D., AND TRUJILLO, M. (1978) Countertransference examples of syntactic expression of warded-off contents. *Psychoanalytic Quarterly* 47:339–63.

DIAZ DE CHUMACEIRO, C. L. (1988) Induced song recall: A diagnostic and psychotherapeutic technique. Doctoral dissertation. *Dissertation Abstracts International* 49, 03 B. University Microfilms International, No. 88-07, 026.

——. (1990a) Songs of the countertransference in psychotherapy dyads. *American Journal of Psychoanalysis.* 50:75–90.

——. (1990b) What else did the obsessive hunter hum about? A contribution to Samuel Juni's case. *Psychoanalytic Review* 77:219–233.

ECKSTEIN, G. (1936) *Canary: The History of a Family.* New York: Harper and Brothers.

EDELMAN, G. M. (1978) Group selection and phasic re-entrant signaling: A theory of higher brain function. In *The Mindful Brain: Cortical Organization and the Group-Selective Theory of Higher Brain Function.* Cambridge: MIT Press.

——. (1987) *Neural Darwinism: The Theory of Neuronal Group Selection.* New York: Basic Books.

——. (1989) *The Remembered Present.* New York: Basic Books.

EDELSON, M. (1984) *Hypothesis and Evidence in Psychoanalysis.* Chicago: University of Chicago Press.

EDELSON, M. (1988) *Psychoanalysis: A Theory in Crisis.* Chicago: University of Chicago Press.

——. (1989) The nature of psychoanalytic theory: Implications for psychoanalytic research. *Psychoanalytic Inquiry* 9:169–92.

EVARTS, E. V. (1960) Effects of sleep and waking on spontaneous and evoked discharge of single units in visual cortex. Bethesda, MD: *Federation Proceedings Supplement* 4:828–37.

FARAH, M. J., WEISBERG, L. L., MONHEIT, M., AND PERONNET, F. (1989) Brain activity underlying mental imagery: Event-related potentials during mental image generation. *Journal of Cognitive Neuroscience* 1:303–16.

FECHNER, G. T. (1889) *Elemente der Psychophysik,* 2d ed. Leipzig.

FERGUSON, S. M., RAYPORT, M., GARDNER, R., KASS, W., WEINER, H., AND REISER, M. F. (1969) Similarities in mental content of psychotic states, spontaneous seizures, dreams, and responses to electrical brain stimulation in patients with temporal lobe epilepsy. *Psychosomatic Medicine* 31(6):479–98.

FISHER, C., BYRNE, J., EDWARDS, A., AND KAHN, E. (1970a) A psychophysiological study of nightmares. *Journal of the American Psychoanalytic Association* 18: 747–82.

——. (1970b) The nightmare: What have we learned about the nightmare? REM and NREM nightmares. *International Psychiatry Clinics* 7:183–87.

FISHER, C., COHEN, H. D., SCHIAVI, R. C., DAVIS, D., FURMAN, B., WARD, K., EDWARDS, A., AND CUNNINGHAM, J. (1983) Patterns of female sexual arousal during sleep and waking: Vaginal thermoconductance studies. *Archives of Sexual Behavior* 12:97–121.

FISHER, C., GROSS, J., AND ZUCH, J. (1965) Cycle of penile erection synonymous with dreaming (REM) sleep. *Archives of General Psychiatry* 12:29–45.

FISHER, C., KAHN, E., EDWARDS, A., AND DAVIS, D. M. (1973) A psychophysiological study of nightmares and night terrors: The suppression of stage 4 night terrors with diazepam. *Archives of General Psychiatry* 28:252–59.

FREUD, S. (1950 [1895]) Project for a scientific psychology. In *The Standard Edition of the Complete Psychological Works of Sigmund Freud,* vol. 1, ed. and trans. J. Strachey. London: Hogarth Press, 1953.

———. (1900) *The Interpretation of Dreams.* In *The Standard Edition of the Complete Psychological Works of Sigmund Freud,* vols. 4 and 5. London: Hogarth Press, 1953.

———. (1915) Instincts and their vicissitudes. In *The Standard Edition of the Complete Psychological Works of Sigmund Freud,* vol. 14. London: Hogarth Press, 1953.

———. (1920) Beyond the pleasure principle. In *The Standard Edition of the Complete Psychological Works of Sigmund Freud,* vol. 4. London: Hogarth Press, 1953.

FRIEDMAN, D. P. (1983) Laminar patterns of termination of cortico-cortical afferents in the somatosensory system. *Brain Research* 273:147–51.

FRIEDMAN, D. P., MURRAY, E. A., O'NEILL, J. B., AND MISHKIN, M. (1986) Cortical connections of the somatosensory fields of the lateral sulcus of macaques: Evidence for a corticolimbic pathway for touch. *Journal of Comparative Neurology* 252:323–47.

FRIEDMAN, H. R., JANAS, J. D., AND GOLDMAN-RAKIC, P. S. (1990) Enhancement of metabolic activity in the diencephalon of monkeys performing working memory tasks: A 2-deoxyglucose study in behaving rhesus monkeys. *Journal of Cognitive Neuroscience* 2(1):18–31.

FRIEDMAN, S., AND FISHER, C. (1967) On the presence of a rhythmic, diurnal, oral instinctual drive cycle in man: A preliminary report. *Journal of the American Psychoanalytic Association* 15:317–42.

GARDNER, R., JR., GROSSMAN, W. I., ROFFWARG, H. P., AND WEINER, H. (1975) The relationship of small limb movements during REM sleep to dreamed limb action. *Psychosomatic Medicine* 37:147–59.

GAZZANIGA, M. S. (1976) The biology of memory. In *Neural Mechanisms of Learning and Memory,* ed. M. R. Rosenzweig and E. L. Bennett. Cambridge: MIT Press.

———. (1989) Organization of the human brain. *Science* 245:947–52.

GILL, M., AND HOFFMAN, I. (1981) *Analysis of Transference.* Vol. 2, *Studies of Seven Audio-Recorded Psychoanalytic Sessions.* Psychological Issues, Monograph 54. New York: International Universities Press.

GOULD, S. (1985) *The Flamingo's Smile: Reflections in Natural History.* New York: W. W. Norton & Company.

———. (1986) Evolution and the triumph of homology, or why history matters. *American Scientist* 74:60–69.

GOURAS, P. (1981) Oculomotor system. In *Principles of Neural Science,* ed. E. R. Kandel and J. H. Schwartz. New York: Elsevier/North-Holland pp. 394–405.

GREENBERG, R., AND PEARLMAN, C. (1974) Cutting the REM nerve: An approach to the adaptive role of REM sleep. *Perspectives in Biology and Medicine* 17:513–21.

———. (1975) REM sleep and the analytic process: A psychophysiologic bridge. *Psychoanalytic Quarterly* 44:392–402.

———. (1980) The private language of the dream. In *The Dream in Clinical Practice,* ed. J. Natterson. New York: Jason Aronson.

HARTMANN, E. (1967) *The Biology of Dreaming.* Springfield, Ill.: Charles C. Thomas.

———. (1973) *The Functions of Sleep.* New Haven: Yale University Press.

———. (1982) From the biology of dreaming to the biology of the mind. *The Psychoanalytic Study of the Child* 37:303–35.

REFERENCES

———. (1984) *The Nightmare.* New York: Basic Books.

HAURI, P. (1977) The sleep disorders, 1st ed. In *Current Concepts.* Kalamazoo, MI: Upjohn Company.

HOBSON, J. A. (1988) *The Dreaming Brain.* New York: Basic Books.

HOBSON, J. A., AND MCCARLEY, R. W. (1977) The brain as a dream state generator: An activation-synthesis hypothesis of the dream process. *American Journal of Psychiatry* 134:1335–48.

HOROWITZ, M. J. (1979) *States of Mind: Analysis of Change in Psychotherapy.* New York: Plenum.

HUBEL, D. H. (1959) Single unit activity in striate cortex of unrestrained cats. *Journal of Physiology* 147:226–40.

———. (1960a) Electrocorticograms in cats during natural sleep. *Archives Italienne de Biologie* 98:171–81.

———. (1960b) Single unit activity in lateral geniculate body and optic tract of unrestrained cats. *Journal of Physiology* (London) 150:91–104.

———. (1988) *Eye, Brain and Vision.* New York: Scientific American Library/Freeman.

JACOBS, T. H. (1975) Posture, gesture, and movement in the analyst: Cues to interpretation and countertransference. *Psychoanalytic Quarterly* 44:676–77.

JOUVET, M. (1962) Recherches sur les structures nerveuses et les mecanismes responsables des differentes phases du sommeil physiologique. *Archives Italiennes de Biologie* 100:125–206.

KANDEL, E. R. (1979) Psychotherapy and the single synapse: The impact of psychiatric thought on neurobiologic research. *The New England Journal of Medicine* 301:1028–37.

———. (1981) Visual system III: Physiology of the central visual pathways. In *Principles of Neural Science,* ed. E. R. Kandel and J. H. Schwartz. New York: Elsevier/North-Holland pp. 236–248.

———. (1985) Steps toward a molecular grammar for learning: Explorations into the nature of memory. In *Medicine, Science, and Society,* ed. K. J. Isselbacher. New York: John Wiley.

KANDEL, E. R., AND SCHWARTZ, J. H. (1982) Molecular biology of learning: Modulation of transmitter release. *Science* 218:433–43.

KANDEL, E. R., ABRAMS, T., BERNIER, L., CAREW, T. J., HAWKINS, R. D., AND SCHWARTZ, J. H. (1983) Classical conditioning and sensitization share aspects of the same molecular cascade in aplysia. In *Cold Spring Harbor Symposia on Quantitative Biology* 48(2):821–30.

KLEITMAN, N. (1963) *Sleep and Wakefulness.* Chicago: University of Chicago Press.

KNAPP, P. H., MUSHATT, C., AND NEMETZ, S. J. (1966) Asthma, melancholia, and death. I. Psychoanalytic considerations. *Psychosomatic Medicine* 28:114.

KNAPP, P. H., MUSHATT, C., NEMETZ, S. J., CONSTANTINE, H., AND FRIEDMAN, S. (1970) The context of reported asthma during psychoanalysis. *Psychosomatic Medicine* 32:167–88.

KOSSLYN, S. M. (1988) Aspects of a cognitive neuroscience of mental imagery. *Science* 240:1621–26.

KRIS, E. (1956) On some vicissitudes of insight in psychoanalysis. *International Journal of Psycho-Analysis* 37:445–55.

KUDLER, H. (1989) The tension between psychoanalysis and neuroscience: A perspective on dream theory in psychiatry. *Psychoanalysis and Contemporary Thought* 12:599–617.

LEHTONEN, J. (1980) The relationship between neurophysiology and psychoanalysis in the light of dream research. *Perspectives in Biology and Medicine* 23(3):415–423.

———. (1985) The psychoanalytic view of dreams and its relations with physiology. In *The Psychopathology of Dream and Sleeping*, ed. K. Achté ja Tamminen T. Proceedings of the World Psychiatric Association Symposium. Psychiatrica Fennica Suppl.: 61–65

LEIGH, H., AND REISER, M.F. (1985). *The Patient: Biological, Psychological, and Social Dimensions of Medical Practice*, 2nd Ed. New York: Plenum.

LIBET, B. (1985) Unconscious cerebral initiative and the role of conscious will in voluntary action. *The Behavioral and Brain Sciences* 8:529–39.

LIVINGSTONE, M., AND HUBEL, D. (1988) Segregation of form, color, movement and depth: Anatomy, physiology, and perception. *Science* 240:740–49.

LUBORSKY, L. (1973) Forgetting and remembering (momentary forgetting) during psychotherapy. In *Psychoanalytic Research*, ed. M. Mayman. Psychological Issues, Monograph 30. New York: International Universities Press.

———. (1976) Helping alliances in psychotherapy: The groundwork for a study of their relationship to its outcome. In *Successful Psychotherapy*, ed. J. L. Claghorn. New York: Brunner/Mazel.

———. (1984) *Principles of Psychoanalytic Psychotherapy: A Manual for Supportive-Expressive Treatment.* New York: Basic Books.

LUBORSKY, L., BACHRACH, H., GRAFF, H., PULVER, S., AND CHRISTOPH, P. (1979) Preconditions and consequences of transference interpretations: A clinical-quantitative investigation. *Journal of Nervous and Mental Disease* 169:391–401.

MAHL, G. F., ROTHENBERG, A., DELGADO, J. M. R., AND HAMLIN, H. (1964) Psychologic response in the human to intracerebral electrical stimulation. *Psychosomatic Medicine* 26:337.

McEWEN, B.S. (1986) Steroids and brain function. TIPS Reviews. In *The Ever-Changing Brain*, California Neuropsychology Services.

McEWEN, B. S. (1987) Glucocorticoid-biogenic amine interactions in relation to mood and behavior. *Biochemical Pharmacology* 36:1755–63.

McEWEN, B. S., AND BRINTON, R. E. (1987) Neuroendocrine aspects of adaptation. In *Progress in Brain Research*, ed. D. DeWied et al. Amsterdam: Elsevier.

McLAUGHLIN, J. T. (1987) The play of transference: Some reflections on enactment in the psychoanalytic situation. *Journal of the American Psychoanalytic Association* 35:557–82.

MILNER, B. (1962) Les troubles de la memoire accompagnant des lesions hippocampiques bilaterales. In *Psychologie de l'Hippocampe.* Paris: Centre Nationale de la Recherche Scientifique.

MISHKIN, M. (1982) A memory system in the monkey. *Philosophical Transactions of the Royal Society of London* B298:85–95.

MISHKIN, M., AND APPENZELLER, T. (1987) The anatomy of memory. *Scientific American* 256(6):80–86

MOUNTCASTLE, V. B. (1978) An organizing principle for cerebral function: The unit module and the distributed system. In *The Mindful Brain: Cortical Organization and the Group-Selective Theory of Higher Brain Function.* Cambridge: MIT Press.

OLDS, J. L., ANDERSON, M. L., MCPHIE, D. L., STATEN, L. D., AND ALKON, D. L. (1989) Imaging of memory-specific changes in the distribution of protein kinase C in the hippocampus. *Science* 245:866–69.

PALOMBO, S. R. (1973) The associative memory tree. In *Psychoanalysis and Contemporary Science,* vol. 2, ed. B. B. Rubinstein. New York: Macmillan.

———. (1978) *Dreaming and Memory: A New Information Processing Model.* New York: Basic Books.

PARMELEE, A. H., WENNER, W. H., AKIYAMA, Y., SCHULTZ, M., AND STERN, E. (1967) Sleep states in premature infants. *Developmental Medicine and Child Neurology* 9:70–77.

PENFIELD, W., AND JASPER, H. (1954) *Epilepsy and the Functional Anatomy of the Human Brain.* Boston: Little Brown.

PENFIELD, W., AND PEROT, P. (1963) The brain's record of auditory and visual experience: A final summary and discussion. *Brain* 86:595–696.

REISER, M. F. (1984) *Mind, Brain, Body: Toward a Convergence of Psychoanalysis and Neurobiology.* New York: Basic Books.

ROFFWARG, H. P., DEMENT, W. C., MUZIO, J. N., AND FISHER, C. (1962) Dream imagery: Relationship to rapid eye movements of sleep. *Archives of General Psychiatry* 7:235–58.

ROFFWARG, H. P., MUZIO, J. N., AND DEMENT, W. C. (1966) Ontogenetic development of the human sleep-dream cycle. *Science* 152:604–19.

ROSS, D. W., AND KAPP, F. T. (1962) A technique for self-analysis of countertransference: Use of the psychoanalyst's visual images in response to patient's dreams. *Journal of the American Psychoanalytic Association* 10:643–57.

RUMELHART, D. E., MCCLELLAND, J. L., AND THE PDP RESEARCH GROUP. (1986) *Parallel Distributed Processing: Explorations in the Microstructure of Cognition.* Cambridge: MIT Press.

SHANE, E., AND KLUMPNER, G. (1989) Meet the American. *Newsletter of the American Psychoanalytic Association* 22(4):12–15.

SHEVRIN, H. (1978) Evoked potential evidence for unconscious mental processes: A review of the literature. In *The Unconscious: Nature, Functions, and Methods of Study,* ed. A. S. Prangishvili, A. E. Sherozin, and F. V. Bassin. Tbilisi, Georgia, USSR: Metsniereba.

———. (1988) Unconscious conflict: A convergent psychodynamic and electrophysiological approach. In *Psychodynamics and Cognition,* ed. M. J. Horowitz. Chicago: University of Chicago Press.

SHEVRIN, H., AND DICKMAN, S. (1980) The psychological unconscious: A necessary assumption for all psychological theory? *American Psychologist* 35:421–34.

SNYDER, F. (1963) The new biology of dreaming. *Archives of General Psychiatry* 8:95–104.

———. (1965) Progress in the new biology of dreaming. *American Journal of Psychiatry* 122:377–90.

———. (1966) Toward an evolutionary theory of dreaming. *American Journal of Psychiatry* 123:121–36.

SQUIRE, L. R. (1987) *Memory and Brain.* New York: Oxford University Press.

STERIADE, M. (1984) The excitatory-inhibitory response sequence of thalamic and neocortical cells: State-related changes and regulatory systems. In *Dynamic Aspects of Neocortical Function,* ed. G. M. Edelman, W. E. Gall, and W. M. Cowan. New York: John Wiley.

STERIADE, M., AND HOBSON, J. A. (1976) Neuronal activity during the sleep-waking cycle. *Progress in Neurobiology* 6:155–376.

STEVENS, C.F. (1989) Strengthening the synapses. *Nature (News)* 338 (6215): 460–61.

SULLOWAY, F. (1979) *Freud, Biologist of the Mind.* New York: Basic Books.

TULVING, E. (1983) *Elements of Episodic Memory.* Oxford: Oxford University Press.

———. (1989) Remembering and knowing the past. *American Scientist* 77:361–67.

UNGERLEIDER, L. G., AND DESIMONE, R. (1986) Cortical connections of visual area MT in the macaque. *Journal of Comparative Neurology* 248:190–222.

WEISS, J., AND SAMPSON, H. (1986) *The Psychoanalytic Process: Theory, Clinical Observations, and Empirical Research.* New York: The Guilford Press.

WINSON, J. (1985) *Brain and Psyche: The Biology of the Unconscious.* New York: Doubleday/Anchor Press.

———. (1986) Behaviorally dependent neuronal gating in the hippocampus. In *The Hippocampus,* vol. 4, ed. R. L. Isaacson and K. H. Pribram. New York: Plenum.

WINSON, J., AND DAHL, D. (1986) Long-term potentiation in dentate gyrus: Induction by asynchronous volleys in separate afferents. *Science* 234:985–88.

Index

Activated sleep, 136
"Activation-Synthesis Hypothesis of Dreaming" (Hobson), 138, 194
Adaptive behavior, 171, 195
Adrenal cortex stress hormones, 125
Affect, 46–48, 52; "dual track approach" and, 168; memory and, 62; mind/body changes, 160; sensory percepts and, 62, 91–92
Alarm, 125
Alertness, 132
Alexander, Franz, 202
Amacher, P., 22
American Psychoanalytic Association, Committee on Scientific Activities, 58
Amnesia, 119
Amygdala, 115, 117, 122–24, 196
Animals: anxiety response, 169; cats, 127–28; hibernation, 130; monkeys, studies of, 99, 105–110, 117; rapid eye movement sleep in, 9; sea snails, 161, 166
Anxiety: automatic response, 169; dreams, 132; dysphoric, 190; signal anxiety, 171

Aplysia californica, 161, 166
Appenzeller, T., 109, 110, 117
Arousal, 132
Artificial intelligence, 133, 164
Association: cortex, 132, 168, 178, 182, 191, 198; free association, 191–92; learning, 164; sensory percepts, links between, 167–68; strength of, 178

Baasch, Michael, 202
Benedek, Theresa, 202
The Biology of the Unconscious (Winson), 120
Biorhythms, 128–30
Botanical monograph dream (Freud), 32–44, 50, 52, 60, 61, 177–78, 183
Brain: cognitive neuroscience, 105–126; images, processing, 97–104; levels of function, 162–65; mind/brain-body, 160, 200, 202; sleeping, physiology of, 127–45. *See also* specific topics
Brain and Psyche (Winson), 120

Kandel, Eric, 163, 202
Kapp, Fred, 57
Knapp, Peter, 202
Koller, Karl, 34, 36
Königstein, Dr., 33, 35–36, 39, 41, 44, 51, 177, 183
Kosslyn, Stephen M., 99–100
Kudler, Harold, 4

Learning, 164; habits, 116. *See also* One-trial object recognition test
Levine, Maurice, 202
Lichtenberg, Joseph, 202
Light, perception of, 98
"Limbic" lobe, 116
Livingston, Margaret, 99
Long-term potentiation, 119–20, 196

Magnetic Resonance Imaging (MRI), 164
Mann, Thomas, 153
McCarley, Robert, 175, 192–93
McLaughlin, James, 57–58
Meaning, 18; dreams, generally, 21–24, 84, 176, 188–94; Freud's dream theory, 26–27; ideation and, 56
"Medial" temporal lobe, 116–24, 193
Memory: affect and, 62; dreams and, 44–45; motor component, 48; networks, 60, 81; organization of, principle, 45–50; psychoanalyst and patient, interacting networks, 58–59, 64–92; psychological field of inquiry, 6–12; sensory component, 48; subjective component, 48. *See also* Neural networks; Nodal memory networks
Menninger, Karl, 202
Menstrual cycle, 130
Mind/brain-body, 160, 200, 202
Mirsky, Arthur, 202
Mishkin, Mortimer, 105–110, 117, 163, 202

Mitchison, Graeme, 17
Mnemic images, 177, 189–90, 191
Monkeys, studies of, 99, 105–110, 117
Mood: role in dreams, 73–75; seasonal variations, 130
Motor phenomena, 57–58
Mountcastle, V. B., 160
MRI. *See* Magnetic Resonance Imaging (MRI)
Muscle relaxation, 136
Muzio, Joseph, 183, 194–95

National Institute of Mental Health (NIMH), 105, 110
Neocortex, 7
Neonates, 194, 195
"Neural Darwinism," 155
Neural nets, 163–64
Neural networks, 158, 164–65, 167, 171
Neuroendocrine activation, 48
Neuromodulators, 179
Neurons, 155, 161, 178–79
Neuroscience and dreams, 95–145; cognitive neuroscience research, 108–110; The one-trial object recognition test, 105–110
Neuroscience and psychology, 55–57
Neuroses, formation of, 189
Neurotransmitters, 121, 124, 161, 166, 179
NIMH. *See* National Institute of Mental Health (NIMH)
Nodal memory networks: botanical monograph dream and, 50–53, 61–62; concept of, 171; condensation, 49; images in dreams, 175; linear arrangements in memory zone, substitute for, 199; mind function and, 164–65; neural memory networks and, 158, 172; perceptual residues, 5; postulate of, 50–53, 59; sensory percepts, associative links between, 167–68; summary of, 91–92
Non-dreaming sleep (NREM), 129